Thematic Unit
Transcontinental Railroad

Written by Mary Ellen Sterling
Illustrated by Keith Vasconcelles

Teacher Created Materials, Inc.
P.O. Box 1040
Huntington Beach, CA 92647
©1993 Teacher Created Materials, Inc.
Made in U.S.A.

ISBN-1-55734-295-4

Table of Contents

Introduction **3**

Death of the Iron Horse by Paul Goble (Bradbury Press, 1987) **5**
(Available in Canada and Australia from Macmillan; UK, Collier Macmillan)

Summary—Sample Plan—Overview of Activities—I Used To Think...—Building Vocabulary—Categories—Multiple Meanings—Scavenger Hunt—Reading Strategies—Sample Webs and Storylines—Inferences—Problems and Solutions—Creative Writing—Discussions—Provisions on Board—Story Events—Attention to Detail—The Real Story—Inside a Steam Locomotive—Steam Engine Flow Chart

The Transcontinental Railroad by Marilyn Miller (Silver Burdett, 1986) **29**
(Available in Canada from Silver Burdett and Ginn; UK Intercontinental Book; Australia, Simon and Schuster)

Summary—Sample Plan—Overview of Activities—Pre and Post Test—Lesson Plans—Definitions—U.S. Rail Lines—Railroad Tidbits—Transcontinental Math—Math Provisions—A Comparison—Central vs. Union—Results—Railroad Time Line—Judah's Dream Game Board—People, Places, and Things

Across the Curriculum **53**

Language Arts: Railroad Word Banks—On the Creative Side—Wheel Codes

Math: Impossible Math—Greater Than or Less Than—Graphic Examples—Standard Time

Science: Train Power—Electric Ideas—Freight Cars—Signs and Signals

Social Studies: Train Trivia—The Underground Railroad—Important Railroad People—Research This

Art: Shape Locomotive

Life Skills: Working on the Railroad—Railroad Songs

Unit Management **72**

Bulletin Board Ideas—U.S. Map—Awards

Answer Key **78**

Bibliography **80**

Introduction

Transcontinental Railroad contains a captivating, whole language, thematic unit about the building of the transcontinental railroad. Its 80 exciting pages are filled with a wide variety of lesson ideas and reproducible pages designed for use with intermediate and junior high school students. At its core are two high-quality children's literature selections, *Death of the Iron Horse* and *The Transcontinental Railroad*. For each of these books, activities are included which set the stage for reading, encourage the enjoyment of the book, and extend the concepts gained. In addition, the theme is connected to the curriculum with activities in language arts (including writing suggestions), math, science, social studies, art, music, and life skills. Many of these activities encourage cooperative learning. Suggestions for bulletin boards are additional time savers for the busy teacher. Furthermore, directions for student-created Big Books and a culminating activity, which allow students to synthesize their knowledge in order to produce products that can be shared beyond the classroom, highlight this very complete teacher resource.

This thematic unit includes:

❑ **Literature selections**—summaries of two children's books with related lessons (complete with reproducible pages) that cross the curriculum

❑ **Language experience and writing ideas**—suggestions as well as activities across the curriculum, including Big Books

❑ **Bulletin board ideas**—suggestions and plans for student-created and/or interactive bulletin boards

❑ **Homework suggestions**—extending the unit to the child's home

❑ **Curriculum connections**—in language arts, math, science, art, music, and life skills such as cooking, and physical education

❑ **Group projects**—to foster cooperative learning

❑ **Culminating activities**—which require students to synthesize their learning to produce a product or engage in an activity that can be shared with others

❑ **A bibliography**—suggesting additional literature and nonfiction books on the theme

---

To keep this valuable resource intact so it can be used year after year, you may wish to punch holes in the pages and store them in a three-ring binder.

Introduction *(cont.)*

Why Whole Language?

A whole language approach involves children in using all modes of communication: reading, writing, listening, observing, illustrating, experiencing, and doing. Communication skills are interconnected and integrated into lessons that emphasize the whole of language rather than isolating its parts. The lessons revolve around selected literature. Reading is not taught as a separate subject from writing and spelling, for example. A child reads, writes (spelling appropriately for his/her level), speaks, listens, etc., in response to a literature experience introduced by the teacher. In this way, language skills grow naturally, stimulated by involvement and interest in the topic at hand.

Why Thematic Planning?

One very useful tool for implementing an integrated whole language program is thematic planning. By choosing a theme with correlating literature selections for a unit of study, a teacher can plan activities throughout the day that lead to a cohesive, in-depth study of the topic. Students will be practicing and applying their skills in meaningful contexts. Consequently, they will tend to learn and retain more. Both teachers and students will be freed from a day that is broken into unrelated segments of isolated drill and practice.

Why Cooperative Learning?

Besides academic skills and content, students need to learn social skills. No longer can this area of development be taken for granted. Students must learn to work cooperatively in groups in order to function well in modern society. Group activities should be a regular part of school life, and teachers should consciously include social objectives as well as academic objectives in their planning. For example, a group working together to solve a problem may need to select a leader. The teacher should make clear to the students and monitor the qualities of good leader-follower group interaction just as he/she would state and monitor the academic goals of the project.

Why Big Books?

An excellent cooperative, whole language activity is the production of Big Books. Groups of students, or the whole class, can apply their language skills, content knowledge, and creativity to produce a Big Book that can become a part of the classroom library to be read and reread. These books make excellent culminating projects for sharing beyond the classroom with parents, librarians, other classes, etc. Big Books can be produced in many ways, and this thematic unit book includes directions for at least one method you may choose.

Death of the Iron Horse

by Paul Goble

Summary

For years, the white men had advanced on Native American soil, attacking tipi villages and taking their land. Now they were building railroads across the prairie. When the natives first saw locomotives they were fearful because they were not sure what this "monster" was. They called it Iron Horse.

One day a group of young warriors decided to protect their people from the approaching "monster." They set out to search for it and after a day and a half journey, spotted the locomotive rails. When darkness settled in they rode to the tracks. Armed only with tomahawks and knives, they chopped ties and hacked out spikes. At dawn the train was greeted with a round of arrows, and suddenly the train cars slammed into one another. Iron Horse was dead. The young men broke into the cars, where they found boxes and boxes of items they'd never seen before. Amidst their fun another Iron Horse was spotted in the distance. The braves gathered all the precious goods they could carry. As they rode back to their village, they were content to know their people no longer had to fear the Iron Horse.

The outline below is a suggested plan for using the various activities that are presented in this unit. You should adapt these ideas to fit your own classroom situation.

Sample Plan

Lesson 1

- Construct a bulletin board (see #1, page 6).
- Sing some railroad songs (#2, page 6).
- Pre-reading Activity (page 9).
- Read *Death of the Iron Horse.*

Lesson 2

- Vocabulary. Categories worksheet, page 12.
- Creative Writing. Choose a topic from page 21.
- Begin Discussion questions from page 22.

Lesson 3

- Scavenger Hunt (page 14 and 15).
- Identify Problems and Solutions (page 17).
- Continue Creative Writing (page 21).
- Word Search. Provisions on Board (page 23).
- Continue Discussion questions (page 22).

Lesson 4

- Research the actual Plum Creek incident (page 26).
- Vocabulary. Multiple Meanings (page 13).
- Evidence. Identifying details to support a statement (see page 17).
- Continue Creative Writing (page 21).

Lesson 5

- Art. Design a steam locomotive (page 69).
- Learn about steam locomotives. Label the parts (page 27).
- Oral evaluation. See quiz on page 25.
- Write a Big Book. Ideas are on page 8, #1.

Overview of Activities

Setting the Stage

1. **Bulletin Board:** Construct a bulletin board using the pattern pieces on pages 73 to 76. Directions can be found on page 72 (#1). Use a push pin or flag pin to denote Plum Creek. Set the stage by reading aloud excerpts from *The Story of the Golden Spike* by R. Conrad Stein (Children Press, 1978). Place push pins or flag pins on the bulletin board to show Sacramento, Promontory Point, and Omaha.

2. **Sing** "I've Been Working on the Railroad." Learn the words to another railroad tune or listen to a recording of these songs. (See page 71 for some resources).

3. **Read aloud the legend** *John Henry* by Ezra Jack Keats (Dragonfly Books, 1965) or the story of *Casey Jones* by Carol Beach York (Troll Associates, 1980). Explain that they are a part of the history of the transcontinental railroad.

4. **Pre-Reading Activity:** Complete the "I used to think..." sections of each topic. Save the papers for later use. When students have read *Death of the Iron Horse,* distribute the papers and have them complete the "but now I know..." section (see page 9).

5. **To introduce the book,** *Death of the Iron Horse,* read the italicized introduction on the page before the actual text begins. Find Omaha and North Platte, Nebraska on a United States map. Discuss the context of the incident with students: the Native Americans were being pushed from their lands. The buffalo, the main food source for peoples of the Plains were being destroyed. A fearsome, incomprehensible noisy moving thing was aiding white people in the destruction of a way of life. With this historical setting in mind, have students read *Death of the Iron Horse.* Copies may be given to each student or to small groups. Or, for older children, type and duplicate the text and have them read it without pictures.

Enjoying the Book

1. **Building Vocabulary:** On pages 10 and 11 you will find a number of ways to build and expand vocabulary. Included with these ideas is a list of suggested vocabulary words for you to use. Add to or delete words from this list to meet your classroom needs. Plan to use a different vocabulary builder each day.

2. **Categories:** The worksheet on page 12 encourages the use of critical thinking skills by examining the relationships among a given list of railroad terms.

3. **Multiple Meanings:** Explore some words that have more than one meaning. See page 13 for a prepared worksheet. This page can be presented orally, if desired. Block out the directions at the top of the page before making a transparency of the text; use on the overhead projector. Extend the activity: with students, brainstorm a list of words that have multiple meanings.

Overview of Activities *(cont.)*

Enjoying the Book

4. **Scavenger Hunt:** This group game will help students review phonics skills and reinforce word analysis skills. See page 11 for directions. Game cards and an answer key can be found on page 14 and 15 respectively.

5. **Reading Strategies:** Ways to increase comprehension skills are outlined on pages 16 and 17. Sample webs and storylines can be found on page 18.

6. **Inferences:** This work page (19) will give students practice with finding evidence(s) to support a statement. You may want to pair or group students to work together on this activity. If preferred, you may present the sentences orally to the class and work on each one as a whole group.

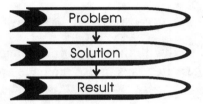

7. **Problems and Solutions:** Page 20 shows a graphic way to identify problems, their possible solutions, and probable results. After completing this page, brainstorm some everyday problems and have the students write various solutions and results. Compare and discuss the different answers of all student groups.

8. **Creative Writing:** The twenty creative writing topics presented on page 21 may be incorporated into your curriculum in any number of ways. Some suggestions can be found at the top of that page.

9. **Discussions:** Use the questions on page 22 for whole group or small discussions. Talk about other questions or concerns that the students might have about this incident.

10. **Provisions on Board:** The names of fifteen items are hidden in the word search puzzle on page 23. After the students have determined all fifteen things, brainstorm a list of other provisions the train might have carried. Extend the activity page with a discussion of which items were probably unfamiliar to the Native Americans. Talk about ways in which the Native Americans might have employed these items.

11. **Story Events:** Group the students and direct them to put the story events in correct story order. Discuss the correct order as a whole class. This page (24) may be converted to a transparency for the overhead projector if you prefer to present it to the whole class at once.

Overview of Activities *(cont.)*

Extending the Book

1. **Big Book:** Cut apart the story events from page 24 and give one to each pair of students. Direct the students to paste the text at the bottom of a large (12" x 18"/30cm x 45cm) sheet of drawing or construction paper. Have them illustrate the text. Arrange the completed pictures in correct story order. Attach to the classroom walls or punch holes along one side of each sheet. Tie yarn or string through the holes to make a class book. (For more book-binding and big book ideas see Teacher Created Material's #133 *Making Big and Little Books*.)

2. **Evaluation:** Students' knowledge and recall of details can be evaluated with the oral quiz on page 25. Complete directions for administering the test are provided. Alternate ways to use the page are also outlined.

3. **The Real Story:** While *Death of the Iron Horse* is based on a real incident, some of the actual details were changed by author Paul Goble. Read the story on page 26 aloud to the students. Follow up with any of the activities suggested there. Encourage the students to find other written accounts of the Plum Creek train derailment.

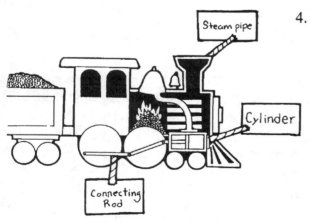

4. **Steam Locomotive:** Learn about steam locomotives. Pair the students and give each pair a copy of page 27. Tell them to label the locomotive as directed. Students may want to consult a trade book for help on this project. Some recommended titles include: *Supertrains. Understanding Trains and How They Work* by Jonathan Rutland (Usborne Publishing, 1978); *Railroads* by T. Harvey (Lerner Publications Company, 1980); *The Big Book of Real Trains* by Walter Retan (Grossett & Dunlap, 1987). Also see page 60 for a steam experiment.

5. **Flow Chart:** Follow up page 27 with a flow chart on page 28. Afterwards, call on various students to explain how a steam engine works.

6. **If possible, visit a train museum.** Arrange for a class field trip to the local train station and a train ride.

Name _____

I Used To Think...

Before you read *Death of the Iron Horse,* consider how you think the Native Americans regarded the coming of the trains. Write your ideas on the "I used to think" lines. Save this paper. After reading the story, you may have formed some very different conclusions. This time, finish the "but now I know" sections for each topic below. Share your statements with a partner.

Trains: I used to think _____

but now I know _____

Cheyenne: I used to think _____

but now I know _____

Soldiers: I used to think _____

but now I know _____

I used to think _____

but now I know _____

Cheyenne weapons: I used to think _____

but now I know _____

I used to think _____

but now I know _____

Prairie: I used to think _____

but now I know _____

I used to think _____

but now I know _____

Building Vocabulary

Listed in the box below are vocabulary words taken from the text of *Death of the Iron Horse*. Add or delete words as appropriate for your own classroom. How-to's and suggestions for using these words can be found following the vocabulary list.

scouts	zigzagged	bound	locomotive
huffing	stingy	spikes	iron horse
caboose	aspects	bolts	tomahawks
ridge	jumble	prophet	unfurling
hacking	hissing	plain	belching
rumor	exposing	panting	bewilderment
horizon	binding	boxcar	foretold
bugle	valley	tracks	incident
smudge	defeated	bundles	dawn
iron	precious	bands	lifetime
images	barrels	camp	jerk
sparks	alight	ties	derailed
awesome	panic	cab	reservations
level	minor	tipi	derailment

1. Type a list of the vocabulary words and make enough copies for each student. Alternatives: Make an overhead transparency from your typed list or the list above; display the words for all the students to see. Write the words on the chalkboard; tell the students to copy the words carefully and keep the list handy throughout the unit.

2. Categorize the words. Group the students and have them think about the relationships between the words and write categories for them. Sample categories include: Sounds (hissing, belching, huffing); Train Terms (caboose, locomotive, cab); Land Forms (plain, valley, ridge). In small groups compare how words were categorized. (A sample worksheet emphasizing categorizing skills can be found on page 12.)

3. Find the root words of the vocabulary words. Direct the students to fold a sheet of paper in half to form two long columns. Have them list the vocabulary words in the left column and write the root word across from them in the right column. Use the back of the paper if necessary. This activity can also be played as a whole class chalkboard activity. Call on a student to write a word on the board and then write its root word next to it. Note: Some words may already be in their root form.

Building Vocabulary *(cont.)*

4. Assign each student a different vocabulary word. Direct him/her to find the assigned word within the text of *Death of the Iron Horse* and to copy the whole sentence in which it appears. When all students have found their words, choose one word from the list. The student with that word may stand and read the sentence. Discuss its meaning based on context clues.

5. Discuss words that have more than one meaning. Write some examples on the chalkboard or chart paper, for example: saw, iron, and bat. Establish that saw could be a tool, a verb that is the past tense of see, or a verb meaning to cut through. Repeat the process for other examples, if necessary. Pair the students and direct them to identify and list all the vocabulary words that have multiple meanings. Encourage students to illustrate the different meanings (see illustration). Follow up with the Multiple Meanings worksheet on page 13.

bat or bat

6. Review and reinforce phonics and word analysis skills with a vocabulary "scavenger" hunt. Divide the students into groups of three or four. Provide each group with a copy of the vocabulary words and a different list of questions about the words (page 14 contains a number of samples to use). Instruct the groups to find appropriate answers from the vocabulary list. They may use a word once for all five statements within a box. Make sure the answers are recorded on a separate sheet of paper and that the letter of their list is written at the top of their paper. As groups finish they must raise their hands. Quickly check their work and have them make necessary corrections immediately. Exchange the scavenger lists and repeat the procedure. Continue in this manner until all groups have completed each list. An answer key can be found on page 15.

7. Keep score during the scavenger hunt, outlined above in number 6, to motivate students and increase competitiveness. Give twenty points to each group that correctly answered their scavenger list on the first try. Give a group ten points if corrections had to be made. Then assign points according to the order in which the groups completed their lists. For example, the first finishers may get fifteen points, second finishers earn ten points, third place earns five points, and all others gain two points. (Construct a scoring system of your own if the suggested one does not meet your goals or purposes.) Record scores on the chalkboard. Provide appropriate awards—stickers, extra free time, award certificates. (See page 77 for samples.)

8. Extend the scavenger hunt idea. Have pairs of students write two or three new questions. Compile all the questions into one worksheet (check for duplicate questions). Present the questions orally to the class. Afterwards exchange papers for correction.

Categories

Words can often be grouped together because of the relationship between them. For example, caboose, flatcar, and hopper can be categorized under the heading Railroad Cars because each one names a type of railroad car.

Study the words in the box below. Decide which ones are best suited for the categories named. Write the words on the correct lines.

Southern Pacific	engineer	diesel	steam whistle
steam	cowcatcher	Santa Fe	brakeman
Erie	jet	fireman	Baltimore & Ohio
air brakes	flagman	couplers	electric

Engines

_____

_____

_____

_____

Crew Members

_____

_____

_____

_____

Safety Devices

_____

_____

_____

Railroad Lines

_____

_____

_____

On the lines below, write your own category and four things that belong to it.

_____
Category Name

_____   _____

_____   _____

Name _____

Multiple Meanings

Some words have more than one meaning or definition. If, for example, you saw the word *bug* by itself, you could not tell whether it referred to an insect, a spying device, an illness, or someone or something that is annoying. Once it is used in a sentence, however, the intended meaning becomes quite clear.

Read each sentence below. On the first line, after each one, write a definition of the italicized word. On the second line, write a sentence of your own using another definition of the italicized word.

> **Example:**   A *conductor* took the train passenger's tickets.
>
> • A crew member in charge of tickets and passengers.
>
> • Water is a conductor of electricity.

1. Chinese crews used explosives to blast *beds* for the rails.

   beds: _____

   _____

2. A golden *spike* was used to complete the Central Pacific and the Union Pacific tracks in Utah.

   spike: _____

   _____

3. Diesel-electric engines have replaced steam engines on most *major* U.S. freight rail lines.

   major: _____

   _____

4. Refrigerator cars carry products that must be kept *cool* or frozen.

   cool: _____

   _____

5. Strong chains and ropes *anchor* cargo securely to the flatcar platform.

   anchor: _____

   _____

6. A tank car is a big metal *can* with a special lining for a particular kind of cargo.

   can: _____

   _____

7. Today, computers are used to help run trains and *check* cargo.

   check: _____

   _____

Scavenger Hunt

Turn to page 11 for directions on using this page. Cut apart the boxes on the bold lines.

A

1. Write one word that begins and ends with the same letter.
2. Write two compound words.
3. Write two words with four syllables.
4. Write one word that contains a silent *e*.
5. Write one word with a short *i* sound as in *ignore*.

B

1. Write one word that contains double vowels (*ee*, *aa*, etc.).
2. Write two words that end with two consonants other than *ng*.
3. Write one word that contains the same short *a* sound as *bag*.
4. Write two words that contain *ou*.
5. Write one word that ends with *ts*.

C

1. Write one word that ends in a vowel other than *e*.
2. Write two words that end with *or*.
3. Write one word that contains the same vowel 3 times.
4. Write one word whose main accent is on the third syllable.
5. Write two words that have only one syllable.

D

1. Write one word that has exactly six letters.
2. Write one word that begins with a consonant blend (*tr*, *st*, etc.).
3. Write two words that end in *ing*.
4. Write 2 words that contain only one vowel.
5. Write one word that has more than 9 letters.

E

1. Write one word that uses the same vowel twice.
2. Write one word with a prefix.
3. Write two words that end in *ent*.
4. Write one word that begins with a vowel.
5. Write two words that have three syllables.

F

1. Write two words that contain the same number of letters in both syllables.
2. Write one word that has exactly ten letters.
3. Write one word that begins with a hard *c* sound.
4. Write two words that end in *me*.
5. Write one word that has a long *u* sound.

G

1. Write two words that end in *le*.
2. Write one word that contains double consonants (*bb*, *rr*, etc.).
3. Write two words that end in *ed*.
4. Write one word in which the main accent is on the 2nd syllable.
5. Write one word that has a long *o* sound.

H

1. Write two words with suffixes other than *ing*.
2. Write one word that ends with *y*.
3. Write two words that contain four different vowels.
4. Write one word with a short *u* sound.
5. Write one word that ends in *ge*.

I

1. Write one word that has both a suffix and a prefix.
2. Write two words that contain three syllables.
3. Write one word that ends in *ts*.
4. Write two words that have a short *e* sound as in *pest*.
5. Write one word that has a hard *c* sound as in *picnic*.

Scavenger Hunt Answer Key

See page 11 for directions on how to use this page. These are sample answers only; you may need to determine the appropriateness of some responses.

A

1. level, sparks, scouts, rumor, defeated, spikes,
2. awesome, alight, boxcar, foretold, lifetime
3. locomotive, bewilderment, reservations
4. caboose, ridge, bugle, smudge, awesome, spikes, ties, locomotive, foretold, lifetime
5. ridge, images, zigzagged, stingy, hissing, panic, incident

B

1. caboose
2. scouts, sparks, aspects, barrels, alight, bound, bolts, tracks, bands, camp, tomahawks, bewilderment, foretold, incident, dawn, jerk, reservations, derailment
3. hacking, zigzagged, aspects, valley, panic, panting, tracks, bands, camp, cab
4. scouts, precious, bound
5. scouts, aspects

C

1. tipi
2. rumor, minor
3. defeated, locomotive, bewilderment
4. locomotive, reservations
5. scouts, ridge, smudge, sparks, bound, spikes, bolts, plain, tracks, bands, camp, ties, cab, dawn, jerk

D

1. scouts, smudge, images, sparks, stingy, jumble, valley, alight, spikes, boxcar, tracks
2. scouts, smudge, sparks, stingy, precious, spikes, prophet, plain, tracks
3. huffing, hacking, hissing, exposing, binding, panting, unfurling
4. sparks, stingy, bolts, bands, camp, cab, dawn, jerk
5. locomotive, bewilderment, reservations, derailment

E

1. level, hissing, binding, tipi,
2. exposing, defeated, alight, unfurling, derailed, derailment
3. bewilderment, derailment
4. iron, images, awesome, aspects, exposing, alight, iron horse, incident
5. horizon, exposing, defeated, tomahawks, unfurling, incident, derailment

F

1. valley, boxcar, tipi, foretold, lifetime
2. locomotive, derailment
3. caboose, camp, cab
4. awesome, lifetime
5. bugle

G

1. bugle, jumble
2. huffing, zigzagged, hissing, barrels
3. zigzagged, defeated
4. caboose, horizon, exposing, defeated, unfurling, bewilderment, derailment
5. bolts, locomotive

H

1. zigzagged, defeated, bewilderment, derailed, reservations, derailment
2. stingy, valley
3. precious, reservations
4. huffing, smudge, jumble, bundles, unfurling
5. ridge, smudge

I

1. exposing, defeated, unfurling, derailed, derailment
2. horizon, exposing, defeated, tomahawks, unfurling, incident, derailment
3. scouts, aspects
4. level, aspects, exposing, prophet, belching, bewilderment, derailment
5. scouts, caboose, aspects, panic, boxcar, tracks, camp, cab, locomotive

Reading Strategies

Strengthen your students' comprehension skills with the following techniques. Select and use those methods which best suit your classroom needs and teaching style. Some sample worksheets have been provided for use at your discretion.

Semantic Webbing

Purpose: To help students expand their prereading language and knowledge and to help them become good question-askers.

Directions:

- Choose reading material that is at the majority of the students' independent reading level and whose content is familiar to them.

- Draw a web on the chalkboard, chart paper, or overhead projector.

- Ask students to share what they know about trains, the white man, and the Native Americans during the late 1860's. Guide them with questions which will elicit descriptive responses. For example, How would you describe the Native Americans? Record responses on the web. (For a sample web, see page 18.)

- Tell students to describe in one sentence what they think a story with a train, Native Americans, and white men might be about. Write these storyline sentences underneath the web. (For sample, see page 18.)

- Read the story aloud to students or have them read it independently.

- Determine if any of the storylines composed before reading the selection were correct. Have them support their answers by finding the proper details within the reading material.

- Evaluate what they learned in their reading by comparing it to the original web. Create a new web that reflects what they have learned. (For a sample see page 18.)

- Follow up with I used to think... but now I know... statements. For example, I used to think that Native Americans were not still roaming the plains when trains were introduced, but now I know they were. (You may want to use the worksheet on page 9.)

Inferences

Purpose: To help students determine ideas that are literally stated in a selection and those that can be inferred from elements of the text.

Directions:

- Prepare a list of several true statements from a particular selection. Write some statements that are stated in the text and write other statements that require inferences to be made. (See the box on page 17 for sample statements.)

- Explain to students that while all the statements are true, some are written on a page of text and others must be figured out from the context.

- Determine which statements are literal, that is, found directly in the text. Focusing on one statement at a time, direct the students to read from the text the sentence in which the statement appears.

Reading Strategies *(cont.)*

- Read the inferred statements and have the students find statements in the text that support these statements.

- Move on to the next step when students are comfortable with the process.

- Prepare some statements from the text which are true and supportable and others that are false and unsupported by the text. (See the box below.) Discuss the difference between the two types of statements.

- Follow up with the Inference worksheet on page 19.

Literal Statement: People feared the Iron Horse, even though they'd never seen it. ("People had terrifying images in their minds. Was it an enormous snake or even an underwater monster...?")

Inferred Statement: The warriors were a determined group. ("With only tomahawks and knives it seemed an impossible task. But they dug down and chopped the ties...")

False or Unsupported Statement: The white men found all the money that the warriors had scattered. (The train was set on fire so probably a lot of money was burned.)

Problems/Solutions

Purpose: To identify the problems faced in a selection and how they were solved.

Directions:

- Present a story problem to the class. For example, "The soldiers have defeated us and taken everything that we had, and made us poor. We have no more time to play games around camp. Let us go and try to turn back this Iron Horse."
- Discuss how the men solved the problem; what were the results?
- Determine some other solutions that the men might have implemented. What might the results have been?
- Construct a chart of problems and their possible solutions. (See sample on page 20.)

Evidence

Purpose: To identify details which support a statement.

Directions:

- Write a statement on the chalkboard.
- Ask students to find evidence from the text that supports this statement.
- Record proper responses on lines below the initial statement.
- Prepare other statements and present them to the students.

Sample Webs and Storylines

Prereading Web

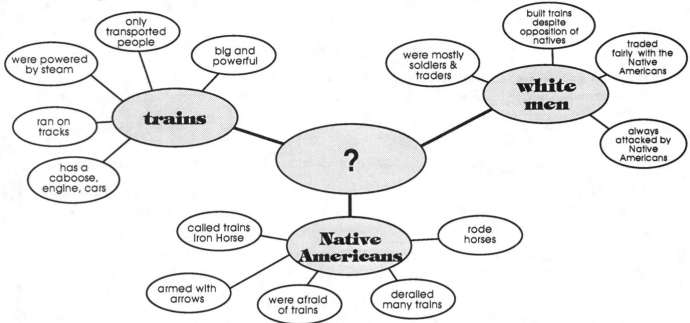

Postreading Web

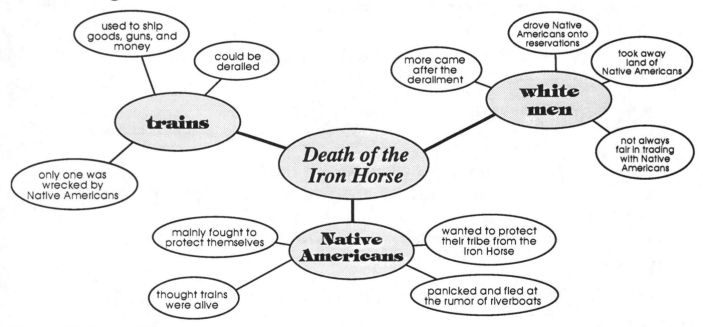

Sample Storylines

1. This story is about soldiers who build a train through land where Native Americans lived.

2. The story is about Native Americans who opposed the soldiers; a fight ensues.

3. This story tells about a time when the Native Americans tried to stop the soldiers from building the train through their territory.

Note: The webs and storylines are examples only. Every group brainstorming session will produce different results.

Name _____

Inferences

When you read a selection, you sometimes make inferences, or guesses, based on evidence from the pictures and/or text. In *Death of the Iron Horse*, for example, you can infer that the story takes place prior to 1900. First, the pictures of the train itself show an early steam engine. Second, Native Americans no longer ride the plains on horseback nor are there numerous tipi villages, so it must take place in an earlier era. You may be able to think of other evidences to support the inferred statement.

Read each sentence below. On the lines that follow, write one (or more) example from the text to support the inference.

1. The soldiers did not respect the property rights of the Native Americans.

   _____

   _____

2. The Native Americans could be playful.

   _____

   _____

3. The warriors were thoughtful.

   _____

   _____

4. The Native Americans thought the Iron Horse was alive.

   _____

   _____

5. White men thought the trains were safe from harm.

   _____

   _____

6. The warriors acted bravely against the moving Iron Horse.

   _____

   _____

7. Derailing the train did not solve the problem.

   _____

   _____

8. The Native Americans were ill-equipped for the job.

   _____

   _____

Name _____

Problems and Solutions

In *Death of the Iron Horse*, the Cheyenne faced a problem: Should they let the white men continue to build railroads across their land or should they take action against them? A young group of warriors decided to stop the Iron Horse by chopping ties and hacking out spikes. The result was they derailed the train and took many different items from the cars. In the end it didn't solve anything because more trains arrived along with soldiers and horses.

The above problem with its solution and results can be illustrated with the following outline. Complete the solution and results for the other problems below.

Problem

1. The Native Americans didn't want the white men to continue building railroads on their land.

2. Soldiers attacked and burned the tipi village.

3. The young men saw the iron bands which bound Mother earth.

4. They found a heavy tin box which would not open.

5. After they had derailed the train, the men noticed another train approaching.

Solution

A group of warriors chopped ties and hacked spikes of the railroad tracks.

Results

The train was derailed. More trains and soldiers came to the territory.

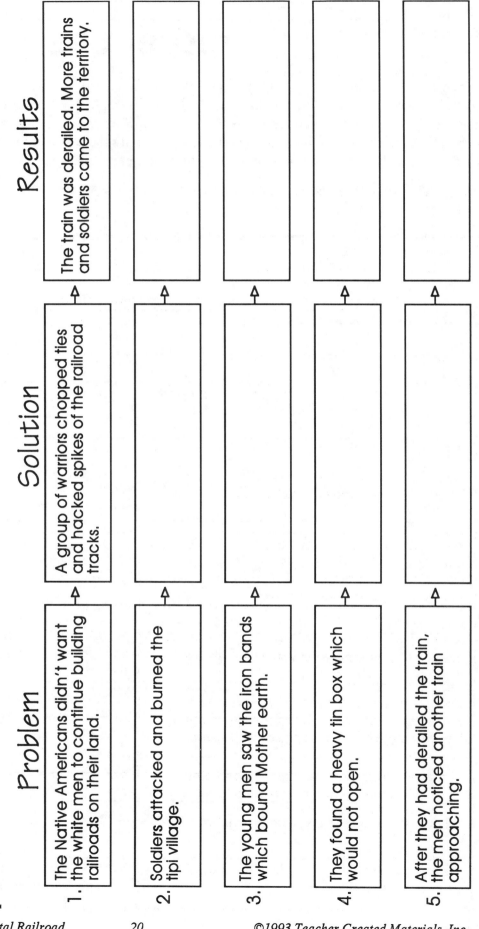

Creative Writing

Present these topics to students in a number of ways.

1. Assign one each day for a daily writing assignment.
2. Write two or three topics on the board; let students choose which topic to use.
3. Give each student a copy of all the assignments; set due dates for the assignments.
4. Group the students; assign each group a different topic.
5. Cut apart the boxes below, place them in a paper bag, and have students choose one.

Rewrite *Death of the Iron Horse* from the point of view of the white men.	How would you have protected your tribe against the Iron Horse? Write a different plan than the one the young warriors employed.
You are the engineer of the locomotive. Write a conversation you might have with your fireman when you first see the warriors.	The prophet Sweet Medicine had a terrible dream. Write a pleasant dream for Sweet Medicine. Include events about white soldiers and a train.
Write a list of all the goods found in the boxcars. Tell which items you think would be most useful to the Native Americans and explain why.	The warriors played a game with the bolts of cloth. Create a game for your fellow tribesmen to play with the cloth.
Your tribe has never seen or heard of an Iron Horse, but you saw one while scouting for game. Tell how you would describe it to your fellow tribespeople.	You are a reporter for the *Prairie Times*. Write an appropriate headline and article about the derailment.
Compare and contrast horses with the Iron Horse. Tell how they are alike and how they are different.	Write a sequel to *Death of the Iron Horse*. Tell what events occurred when the other train arrived with the soldiers and horses.
When the men broke open the boxes on the first car, they found many items. Choose one item you'd like most to have if you were one of the warriors; explain your choice.	Compose a poem that expresses your feelings about the derailment of the Iron Horse.
Interview Spotted Wolf, Big Foot, Porcupine or other warriors before they set out on their journey. Write questions you'd ask; answer them as the warriors might.	Keep a three-day journal of your journey to find and stop the Iron Horse. The third day's entry should reflect the actual events of the derailment.
You are a Native American in the late 1800's and you've just seen a helicopter for the first time. Describe it to your fellow tribespeople.	Native Americans gave the Iron Horse human-like qualities. Describe them. Add some of your own.
Tell how the women and children and others react when the small group returns to camp with their goods from the train.	You are a crew member on the train, but you manage to hide from the warriors. Write an eyewitness account of the event.
What does the expression "train of thought" mean? Write a story that explains how this saying originated.	You are a Native American and have never seen a bugle before. How would you describe it? What would you do with it?

Discussions

Encourage critical thinking skills with the following discussion questions. Students may be grouped and each group given a different topic, or you may prefer to conduct whole-group sessions. These questions can also be assigned as written work for student evaluation purposes.

1. Do you think this derailment incident could have been prevented? How?

2. What if the Native Americans had planned and carried out more derailments? How might that have changed history?

3. Why were the Native Americans so fearful of the Iron Horse? Why do you think they gave it human qualities?

4. White men took the Native Americans' land away from them and then forced them to live on reservations. If you were a Native American in the 1800's, what would you have done to prevent this from happening? Could it have been prevented at all? Why or why not?

5. Explain why you think the small group of warriors was or was not justified in their actions.

6. If you were President at the time of the incident, what would you have done to soothe Native American and white men's relations?

7. How do you think the Native Americans of the late 1800's would have fared if they had arms, ammunition, and explosives? Would they have been justified in using those devices?

8. Why do you think there weren't more train derailments such as the one reported in *Death of the Iron Horse?*

9. Why weren't more men aboard the train? How might the derailment been different if there had been soldiers on board?

10. Why didn't the natives take the "bundles of little bits of green paper"? Why did they take the silver coins?

11. What things aboard the boxcars do you think were most valuable to the Cheyenne? Why?

12. Were the overall results of this incident positive or negative? Explain.

Provisions on Board

When the Native Americans stopped the train they wanted to see what was inside the wagons. They broke open the first car to find a jumble of boxes containing items that were mostly unfamiliar to them. Find and circle the names of these items in the word search puzzle below.

```
O L P A N E L I N C S O M O E K T D S A H S O R A Y O E
S T O A Y M U Y B E E I E N Y O E S T O E Y T R A B A J
A N D O N A H O S R O A Y A H O R A E L S V I E R N E S
M A N A N S A S E S H S A B A D O Y I Y O N O T R A B A
J O P O R Q A U E E S S E S M R O F I N U L F I N D E L
A S E M A L N A Y L A C O M P A N I A N O T R A B S A J
A E N L G O S F I N E S D E S E M A N A N O C L A T N C
O M O E S T A S T S T N A P U Y O E S P E H R O Q A U E
T O D O V A B I E N C O N T I G O Y C O I N T U E H S C
U E L S T E K N A L B A Y O N O S E C N C U A S N D O V
S A S A L E E R E S T A N O T A Y N A O S E S I G L O V
A E S A L E E R A N T E S D E I R P T E A T U V I A A J
E A X C O S T A R I C A O D E S L P U E S O J A L A L Q
U E T A U S A B E S C O M O L A E R E N E S P A N O L F
P O R Q U S E S S I N O S A T B E S C O M O L E E R E N
E S P A N E O L T S N U N E C A V A S A S A B E R L O Q
U E D I C S E E S E T A S N O T A C K E T T L E S U S A
N D O V A A S A J V K U G A R D E P O R T E S C O N H L
A C O M P V A N I I A C T U J U E G A S S O F T B A I L
L M U Y B S U E N N O Y A E L E S P U C Q U I P O T R E
N E C E S S I T O K L A T J E M P O R A D A P A S A T D
A A V E R A S I L A S I Q U I E N T E T E M P O R A S D
A T U J U L E G A S C O N N B U G L E O S O T R O S P O
R Q U E E G S M U Y D I V E R T I D O H A S T L L U E G
```

axes	files	glasses
pans	uniforms	knives
jackets	cups	flags
glass vases	hats	shirts
bugle	china plates	shoes

Story Events

Work with a partner. Together, determine the correct order of the story events below. Number the events in the order of their occurrence on the lines before each sentence.

1. _____ Soldiers attacked villages and killed women and children.

2. _____ The men tried to outrun the train on their horses.

3. _____ One group of young boys decided to protect the others from the Iron Horse.

4. _____ A man tried to escape from the caboose, but he was shot full of arrows.

5. _____ Sweet Medicine had a dream in which strange people killed all the buffalos.

6. _____ First all the precious things were gathered up, then they set fire to the train.

7. _____ Some thought the Iron Horse was an enormous snake or an underwater monster.

8. _____ Suddenly the cars slammed together in a horrible, twisted crash.

9. _____ The group rode until smoke was sighted going against the wind.

10. _____ They had great fun galloping over the prairie with bolts of cloth unfurling in the wind.

11. _____ Slowly, more and more white people arrived from the East.

12. _____ They kept the coins, but threw the pieces of green paper into the air.

13. _____ That night they used tomahawks and knives to chop ties and hack out spikes.

14. _____ Scouts rode into camp and tried to describe the Iron Horse they'd seen.

15. _____ Some shot arrows at the train.

16. _____ At dawn they saw the eye of the Iron Horse approaching.

17. _____ The small group left camp without telling anyone.

18. _____ They broke open the car doors and found many different things.

Attention to Detail

Test students' knowledge and recall with this oral quiz. Direct the students to number a sheet of paper from 1 to 25; tell them to make sure they have written their names at the tops of the papers. Read each sentence aloud and allow students time to write *T* for true and *F* for false. You may want to repeat each sentence immediately after reading it. When the test has been completed, review the statements and answers. If a sentence is false, have the students determine how to make it a true statement. Note: You may record the sentences below on a cassette player. Individuals or small groups can then take the test on their own. Or you may want to make an overhead transparency of the text below. (Cover up the answers before copying the page.)

1. Sleeping Rabbit, Little Foot, and Porcupine were among those who set out to protect the village from Iron Horse. *(False; the second name should be Big Hand not Little Foot.)*
2. The warriors were armed only with tomahawks, knives, and bows and arrows. *(True)*
3. Sweet Medicine was a Cheyenne Prophet. *(True)*
4. The Native Americans took the coins and the bits of green paper. *(False, they only took the coins.)*
5. The train had only three white crew members. *(True)*
6. One young man tried to throw a rope over the engine. *(True)*
7. Iron Horse was faster than the horses. *(True)*
8. The group of young men left their village after telling everyone about their plan to turn back the Iron Horse. *(False, they left without telling anyone.)*
9. People thought the Iron Horse might be an enormous snake or an underwater monster. *(True)*
10. All the men aboard the train died from the crash. *(False, one lived but died from arrow shots.)*
11. One train car contained boxes of bugles. (False, only one bugle was found.)
12. One crew member had been in the caboose. *(True)*
13. The group began chopping the railroad ties at dawn. *(False, they began at night and finished at dawn.)*
14. Scouts warned the villagers about the Iron Horse. *(True)*
15. When soldiers attacked the villages, the people fought back. *(True)*
16. Sweet Medicine lived to see his dreams happen. *(False, he died soon after his dream.)*
17. Box cars contained china plates, glass vases, and buffalo robes. *(False, there were no buffalo robes.)*
18. The train line was the Union Pacific. *(True)*
19. The young men had great fun playing with the bolts of cloth. *(True)*
20. The horses were terrified of the train and tried to run from it. *(True)*
21. When the Native Americans saw the train's smoke, they described it by saying that it puffed like a white man's cigarette. *(False, it puffed like a pipe.)*
22. The band of warriors thought it was impossible for smoke to go against the wind. *(True)*
23. After they opened the heavy tin box in the caboose, they found only bags of silver coins. *(False, it also contained green paper money.)*
24. Flags, tall black hats, jackets, and soldiers' uniforms were found in the cargo boxes. *(True)*
25. The group of Native Americans was familiar with all of the items found aboard the train. *(False, they did not know what most of them were.)*

The Real Story

Author Paul Goble states that his book *Death of the Iron Horse* is based loosely on an incident in which the Cheyenne derailed a train. Share with students the real story after they have finished reading Goble's account. Follow up with the activities listed at the bottom of this page.

Note: The information for the following paragraphs was gathered from *The Transcontinental Railroad* by Frank Latham (Franklin Watts, 1973).

On August 6, 1867 Chief Turkey Foot's Cheyenne warriors ripped up rails and fastened a tie to the track with telegraph wire, thus interrupting telegraph service. Six linemen were sent on a handcar to investigate the problem. When the car struck the tie, it somersaulted and the men were thrown onto the prairie. Five men were killed; the sixth was wounded. Miraculously, he survived the ordeal and escaped.

Next, the Cheyenne piled more ties on the track. When a westbound train hit the ties, it derailed. Both the engineer and the fireman were killed but a crewman in the caboose escaped and ran up the track to warn another oncoming train. Meanwhile, the Native Americans broke into the boxcars which contained calico, cottons, bonnets, hats, and, food supplies. The warriors raced across the prairie with strips of calico and cotton trailing behind them.

Activities

- With the whole class, brainstorm a list of ways in which the two versions are alike and a list of ways in which the versions are different. Use the information to construct a Venn diagram or a chart of likenesses and difference.

- Divide the students into groups. Have them pretend they are the surviving member of the telegraph car. Write an account of the incident from his perspective. Use a news story format, if desired.

- Find and read another accounting of this same incident. Some possible book titles to research can be found in the Bibliography on page 80.

- Locate Plum Creek on a map. What state(s) did the Cheyenne territory encompass at that time?

Inside a Steam Locomotive

Name _____

Read the descriptions of the following steam locomotive parts. Then write the number of that description on the proper section of the diagram below.

1. *cab*: where the engineer sits
2. *tender*: car that holds fuel
3. *firebox*: where fuel is burned
4. *boiler*: contains water which turns into steam when heated
5. *steam dome*: steam is forced upwards here.

6. *steam pipe*: steam from dome continues through it to the cylinder
7. *cylinder*: contains the piston which is moved back and forth by steam pressure
8. *drive rod*: moves in response to the piston.
9. *connecting rod*: connects and turns the driving wheels

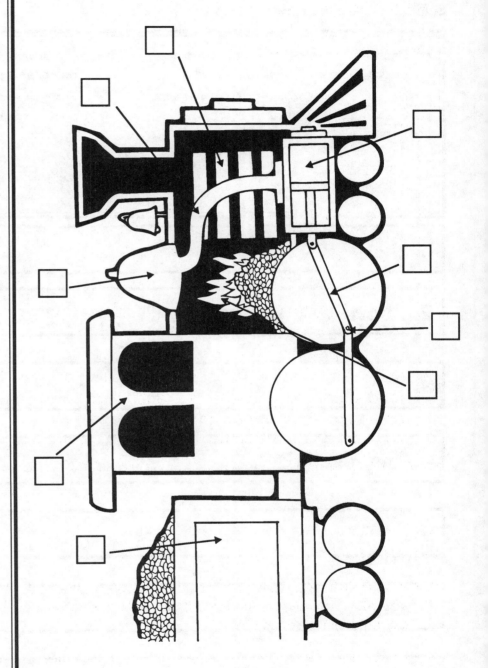

Steam Engine Flow Chart

To learn how a steam engine works, write the sentences below in the correct order on the flow chart. Some clues have been given to help you.

- Once inside the cylinders, steam pressure moves the piston back and forth.
- Heat turns the boiler water into steam.
- First, coal is placed in the steam locomotives firebox.
- The resulting steam pressure forces it into the steam dome.

- The drive rod and connecting rod move in response to the piston.
- From the steam dome, the steam pressure continues through the steam pipe to the cylinder.
- Movement of the drive rod and connecting rod turns the driving wheels.
- Above the firebox lies the boiler with water.

1.

2. Above

3.

4. The resulting

5.

6. Once

7.

8. Movement

End

The Transcontinental Railroad

by Marilyn Miller

Summary

When the steam engine first arrived on the scene, many people were excited about the invention while others were resistant to it. Canal owners were particularly opposed since the railroads could put them and ancillary jobs out of business. Despite many hindrances, men with vision—particularly Theodore Judah—foresaw the need for a transcontinental railroad. In 1863 construction began. The Central Pacific and the Union Pacific faced numerous obstacles including disease, fierce snows and rains, steep mountains, and attacks by Native Americans. But the men persevered and on May 10, 1869 the two lines were joined together. The Transcontinental Railroad *is a wonderful accounting of this event. It is filled with pictures, charts, maps, photos and memorable people who contributed to one of the most important events in U.S. history—the building of the Transcontinental Railroad.*

The outline below is a suggested plan for using the various activities that are presented in this unit. You should adapt these ideas to fit your own classroom situation.

Sample Plan

Lesson 1

- Prefix "trans"; #1, page 30.
- Pre/Post Test, page 33.
- Read Introduction; do activities, page 34.

Lesson 2

- Read Chapter 1; follow with activities, pages 34-35.
- Geography: Train routes, page 41.
- Math Provisions, page 44.

Lesson 3

- Read Chapter 2; follow with activities, pages 35-36.
- Research Projects, page 36.
- Creative Writing, page 42.

Lesson 4

- Read Chapter 3; follow with activities, pages 36-37.
- Venn Diagram, page 45.
- Compare Central/Union, page 46.

Lesson 5

- Read Chapter 4; follow with activities, pages 37-38.
- Cause and Effect, page 47.
- Continue Creative Writing, page 42.

Lesson 6

- Reach Chapter 5; follow with activities, pages 38-39.
- Begin Time Line, page 48.
- Math Word Problems, page 43.

Lesson 7

- Read the Afterward; follow with activities, page 39.
- Review with Judah's Dream, pages 49-51.
- Science: Experiment with electricity, page 61.

Overview of Activities

Setting The Stage

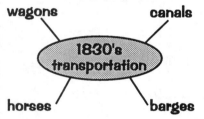

trans
transfer
transmit

1. **Write the prefix "trans" on the chalkboard, overhead projector, or chart paper.** With the students brainstorm a list of words that begin with that prefix. Determine the meaning of "trans" (to go across). Write the word transcontinental on the board. Have the students define it. Write the word railroad next to transcontinental. Briefly discuss the term and some background information.

2. **Read aloud to students the ballad about Casey Jones** (written by Wallace Saunders) or the poem "What the Engines Said" by Bret Harte. (Both should be available at your local library.) Discuss living conditions at that time.

3. If one is available, **visit a railroad museum or a railroad station.** Invite a guest speaker to share railroad information with the students. Check your local hobby shop for possible railroad buffs. Have them talk about setting up and running a model railroad. Students may want to share their models with the class.

4. **Construct a web of modes of transportation available in the 1830's.** Discuss the Erie Canal: What waterways did it link? Why was it important? What other businesses were supported by canals? Sing "Erie Canal." For words and music see *Wee Sing America. Songs of Patriots and Pioneers* by Pamela Conn Beall and Susan Hagen Nipp, Price Stern Sloan, 1987.

5. **Administer the Pre and Post Test from page 33.** Save the students' papers for later comparison and use (suggestions are given at the top of that page).

6. **Read the Introduction of *The Transcontinental Railroad* by Marilyn Miller** (Silver Burdett Company, 1986). Reinforce and extend the text with the activities on page 34.

Enjoying the Book

1. **Assign one chapter of reading per lesson.** Chapter-specific activities can be found on pages 34 through 39.

2. **Lesson Plans:** On pages 34 to 39 you will find suggested lessons for each chapter in *The Transcontinental Railroad.* First is a list of vocabulary words taken directly from the text (see # 4 Building Vocabulary on page 31 for ideas on using the words). This list is followed by a number of discussion questions; answers to these questions are supplied on the page on which they appear.

Then a number of projects are described. These can be completed as group or independent study projects. Use those best-suited to your teaching style and classroom needs.

Overview of Activities *(cont.)*

Enjoying the Book *(cont.)*

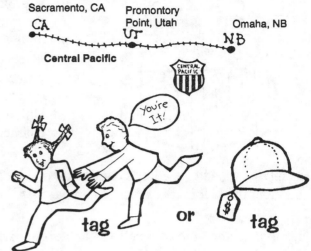

3. **Display a United States map.** This will be useful in tracking the progress of the building of the Transcontinental Railroad. It will also help students identify the states and cities most affected by the construction of this railroad.

4. **Building Vocabulary:** For each chapter a group of suggested vocabulary words are listed. Add or delete to this list as you need to. Employ some of the strategies outlined on pages 10 and 11, if desired. A prepared vocabulary worksheet for this section can be found on page 40 (Definitions).

5. **Creative Writing:** Each day share a different tidbit of railroad history with the students (see page 42). Read the fact aloud or write it on the chalkboard for all to see. Students may write creative tales based on these facts. If you prefer, supply each group of students with a copy of page 42. Instruct them to choose one topic as a group to write about. Have them present their stories in small groups or to the whole class.

6. **Follow Up:** As a follow up or extension activity to #5, above, direct the students to research more information about the event described. Have them draw pictures, make a mural, or write the whole story. Share these in large group. Display them at a special center for this unit; students may browse through them during their free time.

7. **Transcontinental Math:** Two different ways to use this page are given at the top of page 43. It can be used at anytime throughout the unit. Facts on this page will also reinforce what students have learned.

8. **Math Provisions:** This page (44) must be used in conjunction with the chart of provisions which appears on page 15 of *The Transcontinental Railroad*. All of the problems are based on information from the chart. An overhead transparency could be made of page 44 so that it could be employed for a whole group lesson.

Provisions

6	flour	$18.00
400	bacon	$40.00
100	sugar	$7.00
2	dried fruit	$2.50

Overview of Activities (cont.)

Enjoying the Book (cont.)

9. **Comparisons**: The Venn diagram on page 45 compares the immigrant Irish with the Chinese. Both groups worked on the railroad but for competing crews. Find out about them in chapter 3 of *The Transcontinental Railroad*. The Central vs Union worksheet on page 46 also draws comparisons but this one asks the students to identify Union Pacific versus Central Pacific traits and characteristics. It is a good paired activity.

10. **Geography**: After reading chapter one of *The Transcontinental Railroad,* have the students identify and label the landmarks specified on page 41.

11. **Results**: Extend the concepts of chapter four with a discussion of cause and effect. Follow up with the worksheet on page 47.

Extending the Book

1. **Railroad Time Line:** Share the Railroad Time Line (page 48) with the students. In small groups have them construct a time line of important worldwide events. Compare the lists in whole group.

2. **Play Judah's Dream:** This unit review game board (page 49) comes complete with Directions (page 50) and an Answer Key (page 50). Although it is constructed as a file folder game it can easily be made as an envelope game. Copy the game board onto heavy paper or glue to tag board before laminating. Store it inside a labeled envelope along with the Answer Key.

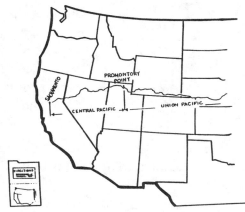

3. **Crossword Puzzle:** Another helpful review method is the crossword puzzle on page 52. Pair the students to work together on it. Or, make several copies, glue to tagboard, and laminate. Place at a special center along with water-based wipe-off pens. Students can work on the puzzle during allotted time. For self-corrections, attach an answer key to the back of the worksheet.

4. **Read *The Railway Children* by Edith Nesbitt** (Penguin, 1975). Compare railroad travel then to railroad travel in the 1860's.

5. **Learn about model railroads.** Two helpful books include *Model Railroading* by Gil Paust (Doubleday, 1981) and *How To Run a Railroad* by Harvey Weiss (Thomas Y. Crowell, 1977).

32

Pre and Post Test

To group students' knowledge about the building of the transcontinental railroad, give them this pre-test orally. Direct them to write their names, the date, and the words Pre-Test at the top of a sheet of paper. Have them number it from one to fifteen. Read one sentence at a time. Tell the students to write an A,B, or C for the correct response. After all sentences have been read, collect the papers and save them. Later, as an evaluation tool, administer the test again. Compare the students' pre-test against their post-test to determine growth. (Answers are in parentheses following each statement for easy reference).

1. General Grenville Dodge was chief engineer for the a) Union Pacific Railroad b) Illinois Central Railroad c) Central Pacific Railroad (answer: a)

2. The scandal that rocked the railroad industry was the a) Big Four b) Homestead Act c) Credit Mobilier (answer: c)

3. One reason the Chinese laborers avoided diseases was a) they worked harder b) they were immigrants c) they boiled water for their tea and rice (answer: c)

4. This man was sent from California to Washington D.C. to lobby for federal support of the transcontinental railroad a) Theodore Judah b) Charles Crocker c) John Stevens (answer: a)

5. The Central Pacific and the Union Pacific railroads met at this city on May 10, 1869: a) Promontory Point, Utah b) Omaha, Nebraska c) Dutch Flat, California (answer: a)

6. Native American Plains tribes saw a reduction of these due to railroad expansion a) horses b) buffalo c) rabbits (answer: b)

7. Leland Stanford, an owner of the Central Pacific, became governor of a) Utah b) Nebraska c) California (answer: c)

8. Railroads became popular because a) they were easy to build b) people grew tired of the canals c) they were faster and cheaper than any transportation (answer: c)

9. The U.S. President who signed the Pacific Railroad Act was a) Andrew Jackson b) Abraham Lincoln c) Ulysses S. Grant (answer: b)

10. Most of the immigrants on the Union Pacific crews were a) German b) Italian c) Irish (answer: c)

11. Railroads played an important part in this war a) Civil War b) Revolutionary War c) Spanish-American War (answer: a)

12. The railroads were difficult to consolidate because they had different a) locomotives b) owners c) gauges (answer: c)

13. The inventor of the first locomotive was a) Charles Crocker b) George Stephenson c) John Stevens (answer: b)

14. Native Americans were relocated to live in a) California b) reservations c) small towns (answer: b)

15. Railroad development in the far west was helped by the discovery of a) gold and silver b) buffalo c) copper (answer: a)

Lessons Plans

The six pages which follow provide a number of suggested ways to present and use the text of *The Transcontinental Railroad*. Each chapter's directions are outlined using the same format. First, a list of possible vocabulary words is provided (for some vocabulary-building ideas see pages 10 and 11). Next are discussion questions—answers are provided for your reference. Finally, group and whole class projects are described. Some prepared worksheets have been included in this section for use at your discretion. Adapt the ideas below to fit your teaching situation. Choose those activities which best reflect your students' skills levels and classroom needs.

Introduction

1. Vocabulary: mingled; detachment; midst; commotion; commencement; unfurl; fashioned; traversed; dignitaries.

2. For Discussion

   On May 10, 1869 "something big" was happening at Promontory Point, Utah. What was it? (The Central Pacific and Union Pacific railroads were finally being joined to complete the Transcontinental Railroad correcting the East with the West United States.)

   "One person in the nation did not celebrate." Who was it? Why? (The widow of Theodore Judah; answers may vary—encourage students to make logical guesses.)

3. Projects

   * Make a list of other important events that were happening in the world in 1869.

   * Direct the students to draw a line. Draw a dot at each end of the line and one in the middle of the line. Label the left dot Sacramento, the right dot Omaha, and the middle dot Promontory Point. Correctly label the Central Pacific route; the Union Pacific route.

   * Find the actual routes of the Central Pacific and Union Pacific from Sacramento through Promontory Point to Omaha. Use Teacher Created Materials' jumbo United States note pads (#804) for this activity, if desired.

Chapter One: "The Road to Promontory Point"

1. Vocabulary: modest; canal; optimism; decade; chapter; technical; initial; cowcatcher; competitors; impede; formidable; opponent; allies; coalition; ordinances; dominated; gauges; incompatible; modes; emigrated; immigrants; famine; trek; burgeoning; acceleration; clamoring; bonds; certificates; collateral; operational; grueling; facilitating. (See page 40 for a prepared vocabulary worksheet—Definitions.)

Lesson Plans *(cont.)*

Chapter One: "The Road to Promontory" *(cont.)*

2. For Discussion

   * Explain the contributions of George Stephenson and Colonel John Stevens to the early railroads. (Stephenson was an English inventor; he developed the first locomotive. Stevens built the first American steam engine.)

   * Name four reasons for the railroad's growing popularity. (Cheaper rates; faster service; could run in any weather; opened new markets.)

   * Why were the railroads important during the Civil War? (They facilitated troop advances; they could transport troops and supplies.)

   * Give the main reason why competitors opposed the railways. (Wagon owners and innkeepers would lose business.)

   * How did the railroad's competitors impede its construction? (They defeated attempts to raise funds; passed local laws banning entry of steam engines.)

   * What groups emigrated westward in this time period? (Germans who had emigrated to the U.S.; Irish who left their country because of famine; New England farmers looking for better soil; pioneers in search of gold and silver.)

3. Projects

   * Group the students and have them draw a map of the United States. Tell them to label it with routes and names of at least ten railroads in existence in 1860. (A prepared worksheet can be found on page 41.)

   * Compare an 1840's map of U.S. railroads with an 1860's map of U.S. railroads. Discuss the changes.

   * Write mathematical word problems based on the information given in the chart on page 15. (A prepared worksheet can be found on page 44.)

   * Look through food ads in the newspaper. Make a chart comparing food prices then to today's.

Chapter Two: "Judah's Dream"

1. Vocabulary: obsession; lobby; secession; swayed; enterprise; provision; homesteaders; prestige; preoccupied; right-of-way; stipulated; contracted.

2. For Discussion

   * What was Theodore Judah's role in the building of the Transcontinental Railroad? (He was a great promoter of the idea; he even went to Washington, D.C. to seek federal aid for its construction.)

   * Explain how the Homestead Act helped the railroad cause. (Uninhabited lands were sold for low prices. Those who homesteaded would need supplies and manufactured goods. A network of railways was needed to transport these supplies.)

Lesson Plans *(cont.)*

Chapter Two: "Judah's Dream" *(cont.)*

* Which U.S. president signed the 1862 Pacific Railroad Act? What was its significance? (President Lincoln provided for two companies to build a railroad. The Central Pacific would begin at Sacramento, the Union Pacific at Omaha, and they would meet at a point to be determined later.)

* Who were the Big Four of the Central Pacific? What did they do to anger Judah? (Big Four: Leland Stanford, Charles Crocker, Mark Hopkins, Collis Huntington. They shoved him aside and bought him out. Then they contracted to build the railroad at great profit to themselves.)

3. Projects

* Examine a relief map of the United States. Have the students determine which railroad—the Union Pacific or the Central Pacific—would have an easier construction route.

* Write a report about Leland Stanford, the railroad magnate who went on to become a governor of California.

* Research the Donner Party incident. Read *Patty Reed's Doll* by Rachel K. Laurgaard (Tomato Enterprise, P.O. Box 2805, Fairfield, CA 94533, (707) 426-3970) for a first-hand account. Another and more complete book on the topic is *History of the Donner Party* by C.F. McGlashan (Stanford University Press, 1940 and 1968).

Chapter Three: "The Great Race"

1. Vocabulary: dismal; coordinated; proposed; grades; flimsily; dormitories; torrential; saplings; ingenuity; subdue; incentive; negotiate; rival; confront; colleagues; recruit; discriminatory; duration; plagued; prejudice; summit; influx; quash; ethnic.

2. For Discussion

* Identify the following: General Grenville Dodge; Jack and Dan Casement. (Dodge was chief engineer for Union Pacific; Casement brothers were the construction bosses.)

* How were the Union Pacific forces organized? (They were divided into groups of workers with specific yet coordinated tasks.)

* "The men of the Union Pacific crews were a mixed lot." Explain. (They were Civil War veterans, mule skinners, gamblers, failed miners, Irish immigrants.)

* What hardships did the Union Pacific crews face? (lice, bedbugs, torrential rains, snow, hostile Native American tribes)

* Why was the buffalo so important to the Native Americans? (It provided them with food, clothing, and shelter, was central figure in their folklore and religion.)

Lesson Plans *(cont.)*

Chapter Three: "The Great Race" *(cont.)*

* What incentives were offered to the Union Pacific crewmen? (double pay for building two miles of track daily; construction of temporary towns after 60 miles of track had been completed)

* What problems confronted the Central Pacific crews? (high mountain ranges; snow; granite hills; assembling a crew.)

* How did the Central Pacific maintain peace with the Native Americans? (gave the Native Americans passes to ride on the trains; negotiated treaties.)

3. Projects

* Design a recruitment poster to persuade Chinese workers to emigrate to America to build a transcontinental railroad.

* Group the students. Direct them to draw a 20 car camp as described in the text. Encourage them to research the topic for more information.

* Compare the Chinese and the Irish workers in a chart or Venn diagram. (A sample Venn diagram can be found on page 45.)

* Read *Buffalo Hunt* by Russell Freedman (Holiday House, 1988). Tell students to write five facts they learned about buffaloes. (For some prepared worksheets about buffaloes, see Teacher Created Material's #285 *Native Americans*.)

* Divide the students into pairs and provide each pair with the Central vs Union worksheet (page 46). Tell them to research information and color the proper railroad symbol for each statement on the page.

Chapter Four: "After the Shouting Was Over"

1. Vocabulary: evident; calculate; influential; disgruntled; aftermath; censured; reaper; volume; exporters; eventual; regulation; subsequent; spurred; resisted; indirect; predicted.

2. For Discussion

* Identify the Credit Mobilier and its owners. (The construction company that built the Union Pacific; controlled by Thomas Durant, Oliver Ames, Oakes Ames.)

* Under what circumstances did Chief engineer Peter Dey resign? (He was asked to make a new costs estimate. The cheaper standards were used but the new, higher estimate was submitted to the government; the owners pocketed the extra money.)

* Why did Oakes Ames distribute railroad stock? Was his plan successful? (To bribe influential politicians to keep quiet about the fraud; no; an insider sued the Credit Mobilier and Congress began its own investigation.)

* Why wasn't the Big Four similarly investigated? (A fire destroyed their records.)

Lesson Plans (cont.)

Chapter Four: "After the Shouting Was Over" (cont.)

* What effect did the opening of the Suez Canal have on the transcontinental railroad? (Railroads would lose future profits since they weren't needed to ship international goods from the Far East.)

* Name four problems faced by the transcontinental railroad after its completion. (High debts; low number of riders and freight shipped; faulty equipment; robbers.)

3. Projects

* On a map locate the Suez Canal. Compare the route from the Far East through the canal and over the Mediterranean Sea to Europe with the route from the Far East over the continental U.S. over the Atlantic Ocean to Europe. Have students measure and compare the distances of the two routes.

* Explore cause and effect relationships. Use the results worksheet on page 47. Or present the information orally. Write the causes in a column on the chalkboard or overhead projector; write the effects in a second column. Choose students to draw lines connecting the proper causes with effects.

* Research the railroad improvements contributed by Eli Janney, George Pullman, George Westinghouse, Fred Harvey, Isaac Dripps, John B. Jervis, Sarah J. Hale.

Chapter Five: "The Road From Promontory Point"

1. Vocabulary: spur; teemed; corrupt; allocated; reservations; relocation; logical; conflict; consequence; endure; circulated; Mennonites; pacifist; persecution; prosper; droughts; hordes; plight; prosperity; stampede; vied.

2. For Discussion

* The railroads helped settle the West, but at what cost to the Plains tribes? (Millions of buffaloes were killed; tribes couldn't survive on their own; they were moved to unsuitable reservations; settlers and miners laid claim to their land.)

* Why did General Custer lead his men into the heart of Sioux territory? What happened at Little Big Horn? (Tribes were fighting back against settlers who were staking claims for gold within the Black Hills which was reservation territory; 2,500 warriors killed every single soldier.)

* Name four transcontinental lines linking the East with the West in 1893. (Southern Pacific; Great Northern; Northern Pacific; Santa Fe.)

* Explain why the railroad promoted settlement of the land along their routes. (To pay for ongoing construction costs.)

Lesson Plans *(cont.)*

Chapter Five: "The Road From Promontory Point" *(cont.)*

* What hardships did the settlers face? (little wood - houses had to be built of sod; floods; hot winds; droughts; hordes of insects; dust storms; blizzards; infertile land.)

* What new techniques did the settlers learn in order to survive on the harsh plains? (dug deep wells, learned cultivation methods from Mennonites; windmills; steel-tipped plows.)

3. Projects

* Design a pamphlet describing conditions on the Plains as they really were. (You may want to re-read the railroad's description on page 55 of the text.)

* Read *Grasshopper Summer* by Ann Turner (Macmillan, 1989) to learn about life on the prairies. Write a story telling how you would have reacted to the swarm of locusts. (For complete lesson plans on *Grasshopper Summer* see Teacher Created Material's #282 *Westward Ho*.)

Afterward: "One Nation, Indivisible"

1. Vocabulary: indivisible; peppered; commemorate; accessible; destinies; ushered; unparalleled fraught; perils; ultimately.

2. For Discussion

* What was the significance of the event of Promontory Point? (Two halves of a continent had been linked making it a nation of "United States".)

* Name three benefits of the completed railroad. (Immigrants from other countries settled on lands previously inaccessible; farmers and ranchers could speed their goods to locations across the country; manufacturers and crafts people could distribute their goods to more markets.)

3. Projects

* Compare a map of U.S. railroads in the 1850's to a map of U.S. Railroads in 1869.

* Read about the revival of train travel in the West. See the May 1992 issue of *Westways* magazine. (Single copies are available. Contact *Westways* directly at 2601 S. Figureroa St., Los Angeles, CA 90007, phone (213)-741-4760.)

* Learn about the high-speed train system being planned in areas of the U.S. Read the article "Rapid Rails" by Christopher O'Malley in the June 1992 issue of *Popular Science* magazine. Check your local library for copies.

* Read all of Bret Harte's poem "What the Engines Said." Assign a small group to find and present the poem to the class. Have the students write their own poems about trains.

Definitions

On the blank lines below write the vocabulary word that best fits the description. Use the Word Box (and a dictionary, if necessary) to help you.

Word Box					
gauge	allies	impede	charter	cowcatcher	optimistic
famine	modest	facilitated	certificates	canal	emigrated

1. The Erie is one; so is the Suez. _____

2. This frame helped keep the train on track. _____

3. Irish immigrants faced this hardship in their homeland. _____

4. Thousands of Germans did this when they left their country for the U.S. _____

5. Some railroads have narrow ones; others have standard. _____

6. These earned interest for the purchaser. _____

7. During the Civil War the railroads made easy or _____ troop advancement.

8. Competitors tried to hinder or _____ the expansion of the railroad.

9. Friends of the Canal Commission _____

10. The speed of Stephenson's steam engine (4 miles per hour) could be called this. _____

11. Many were positive or _____ about canals.

12. Permit that allowed construction of the Camden and Amboy Railroad. _____

Name _____

U.S. Rail Lines

Use an encyclopedia or other text to help you label the following rail lines and geographical features on the map below: Sierra Nevada Mountains; Nevada; Sacramento, California; Promontory Point, Utah; Wyoming; Nebraska; Camden & Amboy Railroad; Erie Railroad; Baltimore & Ohio Railroad; Pennsylvania Railroad; New York Central Railroad.

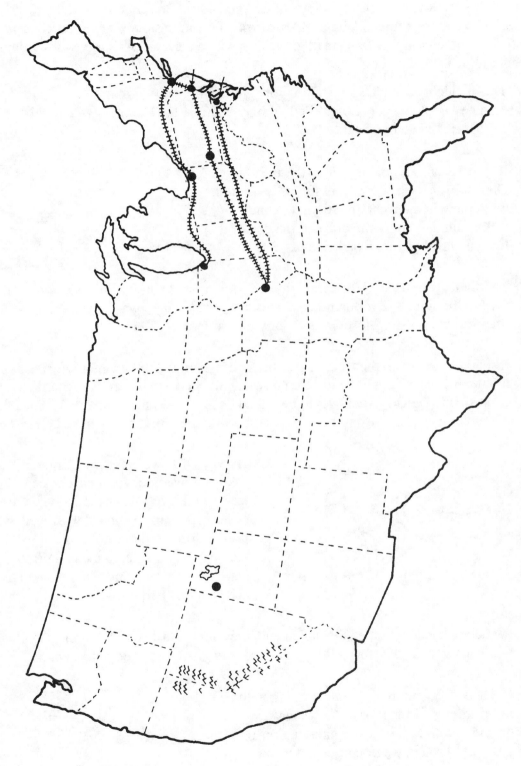

On Your Own. Add 5 more railroads of your choice.

Railroad Tidbits

Each of the following facts are tidbits of a larger story. Present any number of them to the students and have them choose a topic. Direct them to write a creative story about their chosen fact. Share the stories with the whole group, within small groups, or with a partner. Assemble all writings into a three-ring binder to make a class book.

*   This incident took place in 1832 before wide chimneys were in use. A spark from the train engine's chimney ignited a paper bag filled with $60,000 cash. The money—all paper bills—was being transported in an open car.

*   In 1830 a sailing rail car ran on the Baltimore & Ohio Railroad. It was successful only when the wind blew in the right direction. On one run the sailor failed to apply the brake at the end of the line and crashed into a bank.

*   The final spike used in the ceremony at Promontory Point was made of gold. It was pounded into the ground with a silver hammer. Later, the golden spike was dug up. It is now preserved in the Stanford University Museum in Palo Alto, California.

*   Chinese workers on the Central Pacific used dynamite to blast their way through the steep mountains. Men would be lowered down a cliff in baskets from which they would set the explosives. Quickly, they would be pulled back up the cliff. However, accidents did occur. The dynamite would go off prematurely or the workmen wouldn't be raised up fast enough.

*   Harvey Girls were famous for their "cup code." After asking a customer for their choice of beverage—coffee, hot tea, iced tea, or milk—the Harvey Girl would rearrange the customer's cup. Soon a "drink girl" would arrive with the proper drink without even asking. The cup's position was the key. Right side up meant coffee, upside down was hot tea. Upside down and tilted meant iced tea. Upside down and away from the saucer signalled milk.

*   Wallace Saunders wrote a ballad about Casey Jones' last run. It begins, "Come all ye rounders if you want to hear the story told about a brave engineer..." Add your own lines to complete the poem.

*   In 1896 at Brighton, England, a train ran three miles through 15 feet of ocean water. It was outfitted with lifeboats and operated for five years until rough water caused extensive damage to the rails.

Transcontinental Math

All the math problems on this page are based on information found in *The Transcontinental Railroad*. Two different ways to use this page are described here.

1. Copy this page on index stock (available at copy stores); laminate and cut apart. Store in an envelope labeled "Transcontinental Math." Place at your math center.

2. Dictate a problem to the students. Direct them to solve the problem at their seats. (To help you correspond problems to the book, chapter numbers have been provided.)

1. (Introduction) On May 10, 1869 the Union Pacific and Central Pacific met at Promontory Point, Utah. Construction had begun in 1863. How long did it take to build this railroad?

2. (Chapter 1) A 7-hour one-way trip from New York City to Philadelphia cost $3.00. How much was a round trip? What was the average cost per hour?

3. (Chapter 1) In 1840, 2,818 miles of track existed in the U.S. By the end of 1860 there were 30,000 miles of track. How many more miles of track were there in 1860 than in 1840?

4. (Chapter 1) The Illinois Central Railroad constructed 700 miles of track in 7 years. If they had built for 6 more years at the same rate, how many miles of track would they have constructed altogether?

5. (Chapter 1) The North sent 25,000 men over 1,000 miles of track in 12 days. On the average, how many miles of track were covered each day?

6. (Chapter 2) Congress loaned money to the railroads based on the land's terrain. They got $16,000 per mile of flatland. If there were 43 miles of flatland, how much money did the railroads receive?

7. (Chapter 2) The "Big Four" paid Theodore Judah $100,000 for his shares of Central Pacific stock. If each share was worth $4.80, how many shares had Judah owned?

8. (Chapter 3) In 1865 2,000 Chinese worked for the Central Pacific. By 1867 there were 12,000 Chinese workers. How many more Chinese were there in 1867 than in 1865?

9. (Chapter 3) Each mile of track was made up of 400 rails. Each rail weighed 500 pounds. How many pounds of rails were in each mile?

10. (Chapter 4) First estimates of the cost of the track were $30,000 per mile. Second estimates were $50,000 per mile. What was the difference in dollars between the two estimates?

11. (Chapter 5) In 1860 the prairie teemed with 13 million buffalo. By 1900 only a few hundred remained. If 483 buffalo remained, how many had been killed?

12. (Chapter 5) In Kansas 300,000 head of livestock arrived annually for transportation east. At that rate how many would be shipped in 5 years?

Math Provisions

The chart on page 15 of *The Transcontinental Railroad* lists the necessary supplies (and their prices) needed for four men for six months. Use the information on the chart to answer the following questions. Show all work on the back of this paper.

1. How much would one dozen yoke of oxen cost?

   1. _____

2. About how many pounds of nails is each man's share?

   2. _____

3. What is the difference in price between the most expensive and least expensive tool?

   3. _____

4. What is the cost of one pound of rice?

   4. _____

5. How many chisels could you buy with $5.00?

   5. _____

6. How much would 15 pounds of tea cost?

   6. _____

7. Approximately how much is one pound of ground pepper? Round your answer to the nearest ten.

   7. _____

8. How much would you pay for four yoke of oxen and two wagons?

   8. _____

9. What would the total cost of tools be for eight men for six months?

   9. _____

10. How much did it cost to outfit one man for 6 months? Round your answer to the nearest dollar.

    10. _____

11. What would it cost to outfit four men for 18 months?

    11. _____

12. Which costs more—9 bushels of dried fruit or 200 pounds of rice?

    12. _____

On Your Own: Compare the costs of food items then to the cost of the same amounts of those foods today. Make a list of at least five items.

Name _____

A Comparison

Relations between the Chinese and the Irish crew members were not very friendly or peaceful. They were different culturally and ethnically, yet they shared some things in common.

Read the statements below and write the correct number of each one in the appropriate section of the Venn diagram. Use a resource book to help you. (An excellent book for this activity is *Tracks Across America* by Leonard Everett Fisher, Holiday House, 1992.)

1. They faced racial prejudice.
2. They were slight in build.
3. Bosses pushed them to work hard.
4. Fled the famine of 1848.
5. Were Christians.
6. Worked long hours.
7. Often called Tarriers.
8. Many were recruited from Canton.
9. Worked under hazardous conditions.
10. Were efficient, reliable workers.
11. Threatened to strike for more wages.
12. Were prejudiced against non-Christians.
13. Worked with dynamite.
14. Faced problems in their homeland.

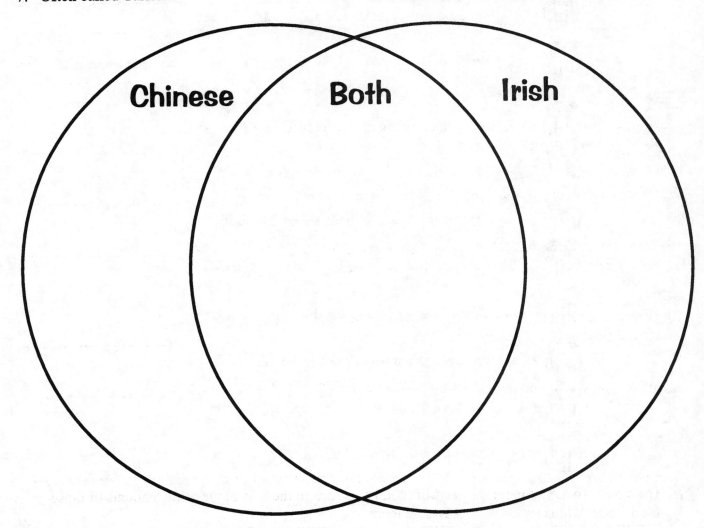

Central vs Union

Read each statement below. Decide if it best describes the Central Pacific Railroad or the Union Pacific Railroad. Circle the proper symbol.

  1. It had difficulty finding workers.

  2. Leland Stanford headed a group of businessmen who founded this railroad company.

  3. The majority of its workers were Irish.

  4. Snow-covered Sierras greatly slowed down construction time.

  5. The Casement brothers offered their men bonuses of $3.00 per day instead of $2.00 if they could build 1½ miles of track daily.

  6. Workers encountered Native Americans and bloody shoot-outs often resulted.

  7. Nine of every ten of its workers were Chinese.

 8. They built tracks through Nevada.

  9. This crew crossed into the state of Utah first.

  10. Buffalo Bill Cody was hired to hunt buffalo to feed this crew.

  11. Most of its crew members drank tea.

  12. Thomas Durant was one of its owners.

  13. Charles Crocker was their overseer.

 14. Construction began at Omaha.

 15. Built ten miles of track in one day.

Name _____

Results

The box below contains ten effects (things that happened). Match them up with the proper causes (the reason something happened) by writing one on each line provided.

Effects

* the value of its stock dropped sharply   * rates were kept high

* Peter Dey resigned   * few people rode the trains

* railroads became safer   * public sympathized with train robbers

* it couldn't be investigated   * future profits were lost

* numerous accidents occurred   * the careers of train robbers to end

---

1. Passenger fares were high; therefore, _____

_____.

2. Railroads were poorly constructed with inferior materials so _____

_____.

3. The railroads couldn't pay off its loans from the government so _____

_____.

4. When the Suez Canal opened, _____

_____.

5. When the owners paid themselves more than the construction actually cost, _____

_____.

6. Because the railroads agreed not to complete against one another, _____

_____.

7. When steel rails replaced the old iron rails, _____

_____.

8. All-steel cars and better police protection for railroads caused _____

_____.

9. After a mysterious fire destroyed the Central Pacific's financial records, ____

_____.

10. Since the railroad's high prices were unpopular, the _____

_____.

Railroad Time Line

Listed below are some important dates in the building of the railroad. Research and find out more about topics that especially interest you. Follow up by making a time line of important worldwide events during this same time period. (A fine resource for this activity is *The Junior Wall Chart of History* designed by Christos Kondeatis, Barnes and Noble, 1990.)

1769: Scottish instrument maker James Watt developed a low-pressure steam engine.

1804: Englishman Richard Trevithick built and operated the first steam locomotive called *Trevithick's Portable Steam Engine* (later renamed *Catch Me Who Can*).

1825: In England the first railroad system—the Stockton and Darlington—opened.

1830: The Camden & Amboy Railroad opened up service between New York City and Philadelphia. Travelers paid $3.00 for a 7-hour one-way trip.

1831: In the U.S., mail was first carried by railroad.

1851: During this year, telegraphs (invented by Samuel F.B. Morse) were used to dispatch trains. Also, the first refrigerator car was placed in service. (An improved version was developed by Joel Tiffany in 1868.)

1859: George Pullman designed and built the first train car for sleeping. His company also designed plush "parlor cars" for relaxing and ornate dining cars.

1868: The automatic safety coupler is patented by Eli Janney; an improved version is introduced in 1873.

1869: May 10, 1869 at Promontory Point, Utah the first transcontinental train was completed by the Central Pacific and Union Pacific Railroads.

1883: Standard time was adopted by the railroads. This concept was introduced by Professor C.F. Dowd.

1886: U.S. railroads adopted a uniform nationwide gauge of 4 feet, 8$\frac{1}{2}$ inches.

1895: The first electric locomotive was used.

Judah's Dream Game Board

To make this file folder game board, copy and cut out map below. Glue to the inside of a file folder; opposite that, glue the game directions (see page 50). Glue a manila envelope with its flap facing you on the back of the folder. Label the front of the envelope Task Cards. Write Judah's Dream on the front of the file folder. Laminate; trim and slit open the envelope's flap.

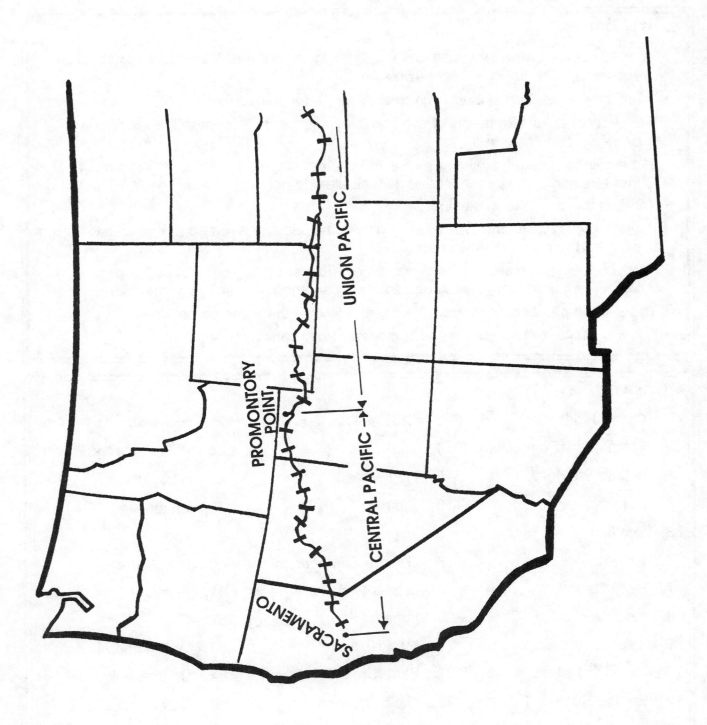

Judah's Dream Directions

Copy the directions below, cut out and glue to the inside of the file folder (refer to directions on page 49). The Answer Key should be copied on index stock (available at copy stores) or other heavy paper, laminated, and stored with the Task Cards for self-checking.

Note: You will need to prepare a die for this game. Cover all six faces with a colored self-stick dot. Label three dots with a 1; label three dots with a 2.

Directions

- You will need a marker such as toothpicks for each player or team, and one specially prepared die with only one's and two's on it.
- Shuffle the Task Cards; place in a pile on the game board.
- Two individuals or two teams of two may play this game. A separate answer-checker may be chosen, if desired.
- Flip a coin to determine who goes first. The other player or team gets first pick of the Central Pacific or the Union Pacific as their starting point.
- The first player or team rolls the die.
- Player or team takes the top Task Card from the pile and answers the question. Return the card to the bottom of the pile.
- For a correct response, roll the die and move forward that many spaces. For an incorrect response, move back one space. Mark the spots on the game board.
- The second player or team rolls the die and follows the same procedure.
- The first player or team to reach Promontory Point wins the game.

Answer Key

1. Crazy Judah	13. Charles Crocker	25. "Big Four"
2. Promontory Point, Utah	14. gold	26. gold and silver
3. Leland Stanford	15. Homestead	27. nitroglycerin
4. Abraham Lincoln	16. Sioux	28. gauge
5. Iron Horse	17. *Jupiter*	29. sod
6. Chinese	18. George Stephenson	30. Bret Harte
7. Suez Canal	19. James Gang	31. Irish
8. reservations	20. buffalo	32. Civil War
9. wagons; canals	21. May 10, 1869	33. Dr. Thomas Durant
10. red winter wheat	22. Plum Creek	34. Colonel John Stevens
11. Engine Number 119	23. cowcatcher or pilot	35. Credit Mobilier
12. survey	24. General Grenville Dodge	36. the Army

Judah's Dream Task Cards

Copy this page onto index stock (available at copy stores) or heavy paper. Cut out the tasks cards and store them in the envelope on the back of the file folder.

1. Nickname given to Theodore Judah.	13. Head of construction for the Central Pacific.	25. Group that financed the building of the Central Pacific Railroad.
2. Place where Union Pacific and Central Pacific met.	14. The last spike of the Transcontinental Railroad was made of this.	26. This was mined at the Comstock Lode.
3. "Big Four" partner who became governor of California.	15. The 1862 bill passed by Congress; provided for sale of uninhabited lands.	27. Explosive used by the Central Pacific for a short time.
4. President who signed the Pacific Railroad Act.	16. Tribe that destroyed Custer's forces at Little Big Horn.	28. The name for width of the track.
5. Name the Native Americans gave to the steam locomotive.	17. The Central Pacific engine at Promontory Point on May 10, 1869.	29. Plains houses made of the grass and roots of the topsoil.
6. Immigrants who made up bulk of Central Pacific crew.	18. English inventor who developed first locomotive.	30. Author of poem titled *"What the Engines Said."*
7. Far East exporters could ship goods through this to Europe.	19. Train-robbing gang of the late 1860's.	31. Immigrants who made up bulk of Union Pacific crew.
8. Lands on which Native Americans were relocated.	20. Millions were slaughtered to make robes and belts.	32. War that lasted from 1861 to 1865.
9. How freight was hauled before railroads were built.	21. Date the transcontinental railroad was completed.	33. Vice-president of the Union Pacific.
10. Mennonite migrants settled in Kansas with gold and this.	22. Settlement where first violence against the railroad took place.	34. He built the first American steam engine.
11. The Union Pacific engine at Promontory Point in May 10, 1869.	23. Triangular frame that helped keep trains on the tracks.	35. The company that built the Union Pacific Railroad.
12. Parties which went ahead and marked the routes to build tracks.	24. Chief engineer for the Union Pacific Railroad.	36. Worked with the Union Pacific to subdue attacks by Native Americans.

Name _____

People, Places, and Things

Check out your knowledge of people, places, and things in the transcontinental railroad era with the crossword puzzle below. Some clues have been given to help you.

Across

3. inventor of the automatic coupler

6. scandal that shook the railroad industry

7. device invented by Isaac Dripps

8. nickname for Irish immigrant workers

9. place in Utah where Union and Central Pacific met

10. His cars made sleeping on trains comfortable.

Down

1. poet who wrote "What the Engines Said"

2. group that founded the Central Pacific

4. waterway nicknamed "the Big Ditch"

5. Bill Cody killed these for their meat.

6. Plains tribe that derailed a train at Plum Creek

Answers

Tarriers	Promontory Point	buffaloes
Big Four	cowcatcher	Credit Mobiler
George Pullman	Bret Harte	Cheyenne
Erie Canal	Eli Janney	

*Answers may be covered before making copies of this page.

Railroad Word Banks

This resource page is a handy reference for various writing activities such as reports, creative writing, rhymes and poems, and social studies lessons. In addition, these terms can be used as spelling word lists and may serve as a springboard for brainstorming.

Important People

Casey Jones	Richard Trevithick	George Stephenson	John Stevens
President Lincoln	Eli Janney	Leland Stanford	Fred Harvey
Charles Crocker	Oakes & Oliver Ames	George Westinghouse	Rudolph Diesel
George Pullman	Peter Dey	Isaac Watt	John B. Jervis
Isaac Dripps	Bret Harte	Mark Hopkins	Buffalo Bill
Thomas Durant	Peter Cooper	Samuel F.B. Morse	James Watt
Kate Shelley	Grenville Dodge	Professor C. F. Dowd	John Henry
	Collis P. Huntington	Sarah J. Hale	

Types of Railroad Cars

dining
pullman
coach
refrigerator
hopper
boxcars
piggyback
tank
gondola
three-level rack
caboose
locomotive
flatcars

Types of Trains

steam
diesel
electric
passenger
subway
monorail
freight
cable cars
suspension
cog
electromagnetic
model or
  miniature

Terms

engineer	fireman	rail
wheel	spike	ties
tracks	berth	coach
Pullman	couplers	cable
flange	cowcatcher	junction
semaphore	coupling	gauge
brakeman	switchman	porters
roundhouse	Zulu cars	conductors
signalman	yardman	torpedo
switchman	repair gangs	

Major Rail Lines in 1899

Northeast
Baltimore & Ohio
New York Central
Erie
Pennsylvania

West
Southern Pacific
Great Northern
Central Pacific
Atchison, Topeka & Santa Fe
Union Pacific

South
Gulf Mobile & Ohio
Illinois Central
Louisville Nashville
Southern Railroad

Great Lakes and Midwest

Michigan Central	Michigan Southern
Central Ohio	Marietta & Cincinnati
Pittsburgh	Terre Haute & Indianapolis
Fort Wayne & Chicago	Ohio & Mississippi

On the Creative Side

Presented on this page are some creative writing ideas that may be incorporated into the curriculum wherever they fit most appropriately. Choose those activities which best suit the needs and abilities of your students.

- **Idioms:** Explore the meaning of some train-related expressions such as, "on the right track," "lost my train of thought" or "one track mind." Challenge the students to write their own train-related idioms. (For more information about idioms see *101 American English Idioms* by Harry Collis, Passport Books, 1989.)

- **Legends**: Read *Casey Jones* by Carol Beach York (Troll Associates, 1980) or *Kate Shelly and the Midnight Express* by Margaret K. Wetterer (Carolrhoda Books, 1990) to the students. Direct them to write a legend about a real or imaginary train incident.

- **Songs**: Learn the words and music to some popular railroad songs. (See page 71 for a sample listing and possible sources). Group the students and have them write a new verse for a song of their choosing. Students may want to write the words and tune for a new song; have them present it to the rest of the class.

- **Poems**: Have the students read the poem "Song of the Train" by David McCord or "Engineers" by Jimmy Garthwaite. (Both can be found in *Noisy Poems* collected by Jill Bennett. Oxford University Press, 1987.) Pair the students to write their own poems about trains.

- **News Stories:** Tell the students to pretend they are reporters for an Eastern newspaper in 1869. Have them choose and write a news story about an event that they think would interest folks back home.

- **Descriptions**: Describe what it might have been like to be a passenger on early trains. Tell about the scenery and sights one might encounter in the West. Explain the living conditions in the workers' camps. Write about the dangers faced by the workers.

- **Words:** Make a list of ten train-related words on the board. (See page 53 for possible words to use.) Direct the students to choose five of these words and incorporate them into a story about the construction of the transcontinental railroad.

Name _____

Wheel Codes

A series of three numbers is used to identify each steam locomotive. This wheel code, also known as Whyte's notation, tells how many wheels an engine has and what they do.

For example, in the wheel code 2-6-2 the numbers tell us the following:

- There are 2 leading wheels, one on each side.
- There are 6 driving wheels, three on each side.
- There are 2 trailing wheels, one on each side.

In the 4-8-2 Mountain locomotive there are 4 leading wheels, 8 driving wheels, and 2 trailing wheels.

Label the train configurations below with the correct wheel codes which are listed in the following box.

2-10-2 = Santa Fe	4-8-4 = Northern	2-6-0 = Mogul
4-6-4 = Hudson	2-10-0 = Decapod	2-8-2 = Mikado

1. _____

_____

2. _____

_____

3. _____

_____

4. _____

_____

5. _____

_____

6. _____

_____

In the space below draw a locomotive with a wheel code of 4-6-2. Write a name for it.

Impossible Math

When Charles Crocker bragged that his Central Pacific workers were capable of laying ten miles of track in one day, Thomas Durant was convinced it couldn't be done. Durant was so certain it was impossible he bet Crocker $10,000. Crocker's crew proved Durant wrong and in so doing set a record that still stands today.

Massive amounts of supplies were required for the day's work. All the word problems below are based on figures gathered from the event. Solve the problems; show all work.

1. Each rail handler lifted 250,000 pounds. If there were 450 rail handlers, how many pounds were lifted altogether?	4. Three thousand five hundred twenty rails had been spiked to twenty-five thousand eight hundred ties. How many more ties were there than spikes?
2. The crew began work at 7 a.m. By 1:30 p.m., 6 miles of track were completed. How long did it take to complete those six miles?	5. If there were 25,800 ties and 3,520 rails spiked to them, about how many ties were there for each rail?
3. In 12 hours 25,800 ties had been laid down. Find the average number of ties laid per hour.	6. The crew built ten miles of track in 12 hours. At that rate how long would it take to build 25 miles?

Name _____

Greater Than or Less Than

Food prices in the 1860's were far lower than today's grocery prices. Use the information from the chart below to help you write true statements. Fill in the blanks with the appropriate sign: > (more than) or < (less than).

Food Item	1860's	Today *
1 loaf of bread	$.05	$1.50
1 lb. bacon	$.10	$1.89
1 lb. coffee	$.11	$2.59
1 lb. sugar	$.07	$.47
1 lb. tea	$.75	$5.70
1 lb. salt	$.01	$.33
1 lb. rice	$.06	$.50

1. Eighteen loaves of bread at 1860 price are _____ one loaf of bread today.

2. One pound of tea today is _____ 58 pounds of coffee in 1860.

3. Twenty-four loaves of bread in 1860 cost _____ 2 pounds of rice today.

4. One pound of bacon today costs _____ 19 pounds of bacon in 1860.

5. One pound of coffee today costs _____ 32 pounds of sugar in 1860.

6. Eight pounds of tea at 1860 prices are _____ 1 pound of tea at today's prices.

7. Three loaves of bread today are _____ 85 pounds of rice at 1860 prices.

8. Eleven pounds of coffee at 1860 prices are _____ one pound of coffee today.

9. Three pounds of rice today are _____ 16 pounds of bacon at 1860 prices.

10. Five pounds of salt today are _____ 148 pounds of salt in 1860.

* Today's prices are approximate. Actual prices depend on the brand of the product and the store surveyed.

Graphic Examples

The bar graph below illustrates eight different trains from different countries and times plus their top speeds. Use the information from the graph to answer the word problems that follow.

1829	1938	1970's	Future Trains

The Rocket (England) — **30 mph**

Stourbridge Lion (England) — **10 mph**

Mallard (England) — **126 mph**

New Tokaido (Japan) — **80 mph**

Turbotrain (Canada) — **170 mph**

Havertrain (France) — **215 mph**

Linear Motor Train (Japan) — **300 mph**

APT (England) — **150 mph**

1. Rank the trains in order from slowest to fastest.

    1. _____   5. _____

    2. _____   6. _____

    3. _____   7. _____

    4. _____   8. _____

2. What is the difference in miles per hour between the slowest and the fastest trains? _____

3. What is the average speed of the four fastest trains? _____

4. What is the difference in miles per hour between the two Japanese trains? _____

5. What is the average speed of the English trains? _____

Standard Time

One of the most important contributions of the railroad to the world is Standard Time. Before the railroads were constructed, people were not careful about the exact time. A typical workday was sunup to sundown; each town would set its clock according to the sun. The result was that the clocks in the next town to the west were slower than those in your town because the sun would be there a little later each day. The next town to the east, on the other hand, would run a little ahead of the clocks in your town.

When the trains came into widespread use, they couldn't maintain a schedule with everyone setting their clocks and watches independently. Professor C.F. Dowd, a principal of a girl's school in Saratoga, New York proposed a method of establishing uniform time. He suggested that the earth be divided into time zones of 15 degrees each. Since the earth is circular and there are 360 degrees in a circle, 360 degrees divided by 15 degrees equalled 24 time zones. This plan was operational on November 18, 1883. Years later, on March 19, 1918 the Standard Time Act made time zones official.

Use this Time Zone Map of the continental United States to answer the questions below.

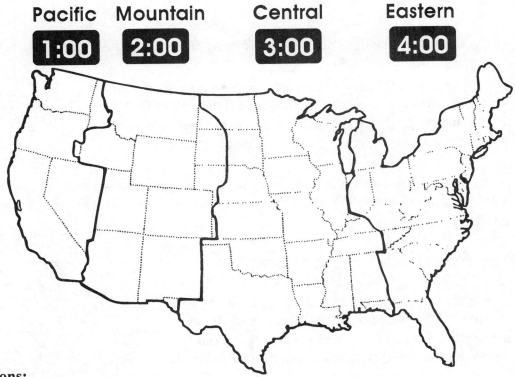

Questions:

1. In which time zone do you reside?

2. When it is 8 a.m. in Eugene, Oregon, what time is it in Deerfield, Illinois?

3. When it is 2 a.m. in Myrtle Beach, South Carolina, what time is it in Dana Point, California?

4. It is 3 a.m. in Butte, Montana. What time is it in Las Cruces, New Mexico?

5. If it is 6 p.m. in Muskogee, Oklahoma, what time is it in Cleveland, Ohio?

Train Power

Early trains were powered by steam, but many of today's train rely on electric power. Explore the properties of steam and electricity with any of the projects below.

Steam

- Pour about an inch (2.5 cm) of water in a teakettle with a pop-up whistle spout. Place the kettle on a stove top and bring the water to a boil.

    1. Describe what happened after the water began to boil. (As the water boils, it produces steam which rises and forces the spout to open and causes a whistling sound.)

    2. Draw before, during, and after pictures of the teakettle during this experiment. Write an explanation of each step.

- Build a model steam engine. Refer interested students to the book *Young Engineer in the Factory* by Malcolm Dixon (The Bookwright Press, 1983) for complete construction details.

Electricity

- Static electricity is electricity that does not move. It can be produced by rubbing things together.

1. Tear a tissue into tiny bits; place them a flat surface. Rub a plastic comb on a wool sweater (or through hair) several times. Hold the comb close to the tissue paper. Observe what happens. (Because the comb becomes charged with static electricity when it's rubbed on the sweater, it attracts the bits of paper.)

2. Put on a nylon shirt or blouse and a wool sweater over it. In a dark room observe in a mirror what happens as you pull off your sweater. (Sparks will fly—this static electricity is caused by your clothes rubbing together.)

- Lightning is also a form of static electricity. Find out how electricity is conducted through storm clouds. (Water droplets and ice particles in the cloud rub together and become charged with static electricity. Positive-charged particles rise to the top of the cloud while negative-charged particles sink to the bottom of the cloud. There the negative charges are strongly attracted to the ground and leap to it as flashes of lightning.)

- Electricity in homes, schools, offices, and other buildings flows through wires in an electric current.

    1. Write a list of appliances in your home and/or school that use electricity. (Answers may vary. This is an excellent homework activity.)

    2. Make electricity. Two easy experiments are outlined on page 61.

Electric Ideas

On this page you will find two different ways to make electricity. Both are easy to create and safe to perform in the classroom.

Personal Batteries

Pair the students to work together on this project. Some supplies may have to be obtained through electronic supply stores.

Materials *(for each student pair)*

- one whole lemon
- brass thumbtack
- steel paper clip
- 2 lengths of electrical wire
- 3-volt (or less) flashlight bulb

Directions:

1. Push the thumbtack onto one side of the lemon and the paper clip into the opposite side.

2. Attach a length of electrical wire to the thumbtack and the light bulb.

3. Repeat the procedure with the paper clip (see diagram). The bulb should light up.

An Electric Current

Divide the students into small groups for this activity. As with the previous experiment, some supplies may need to be purchased from an electronic supply store.

Materials: *(for each group)*

- wire clippers
- 72 inches (180 cm) electrical wire
- bar magnet
- compass

1. With the clippers remove about two inches (5 cm) of insulation from each end of the wire.

2. Make a coil with one end of the wire by wrapping it around your hand ten times.

3. Carefully remove the coil from your hand.

4. With the other end of the wire wrap the compass five times.

5. Twist the two loose ends of the wire together.

6. Quickly move the magnet back and forth inside the coil. Watch the compass needle move.

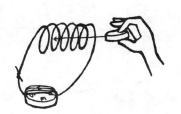

Freight Cars

Connect the illustrations in the center column to the name of the car in the left column and the description in the right column.

gondola

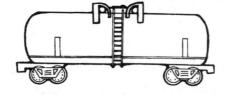

This car keeps goods cold.

box car

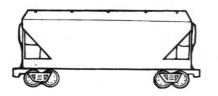

Another open-roofed car; it holds coal and sand.

tank car

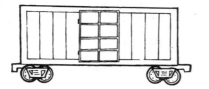

There are no sides on these cars; they carry logs, autos, etc.

piggyback flatcar

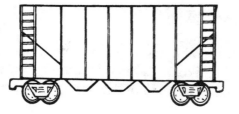

A covered car that carries goods which need to be kept dry.

refrigerator car

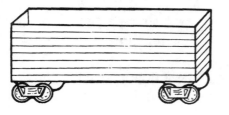

These carry liquids such as oil and gasoline.

hopper

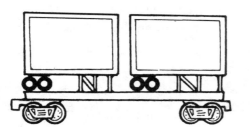

There are sides but no roof on this car.

flatcars

These flatcars carry trailers.

Signs and Signals

Pictured below are some familiar railroad signs and signals.

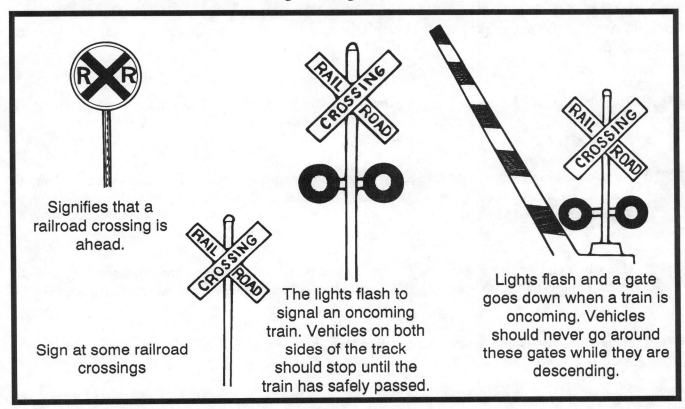

Signifies that a railroad crossing is ahead.

Sign at some railroad crossings

The lights flash to signal an oncoming train. Vehicles on both sides of the track should stop until the train has safely passed.

Lights flash and a gate goes down when a train is oncoming. Vehicles should never go around these gates while they are descending.

These signs and signals are used by the train's crew members.

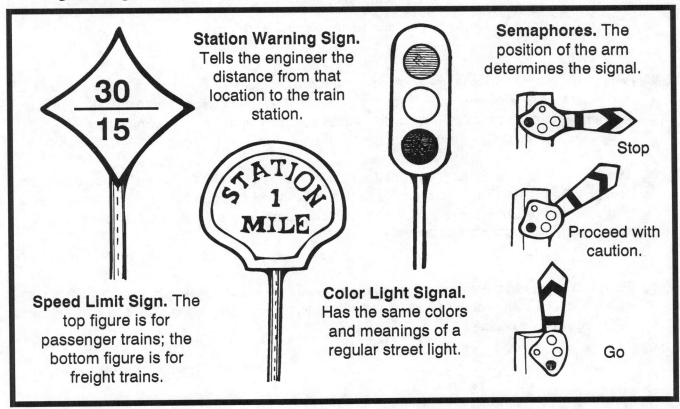

Speed Limit Sign. The top figure is for passenger trains; the bottom figure is for freight trains.

Station Warning Sign. Tells the engineer the distance from that location to the train station.

Color Light Signal. Has the same colors and meanings of a regular street light.

Semaphores. The position of the arm determines the signal.

Stop

Proceed with caution.

Go

Train Trivia

Use these train trivia facts to introduce topics, motivate further research, or entice student interest. Write a different fact on the board each day. Instruct the students to copy the fact in their own train trivia booklet. Add to it as the unit progresses. Encourage your students to dig up other unusual train facts to share with the class.

Since boilers often exploded in early trains, cars were loaded with bales of cotton to protect the passengers.

An 800 foot high suspension bridge once spanned the gorge at Niagara Falls between the United States and Canada. The upper deck was used by trains while its lower deck was a highway for wagons and pedestrians.

One silver and one gold spike were hammered in place as the two railroad lines were connected at Promontory, Utah on May 10, 1869. Later, the gold spike was replaced with a regular one.

Gauge, the distance between tracks, varied among the many railroad systems. Some were 5 ¼" while others were 4' ½". The Erie Railroad had the widest gauge of all at 6'.

Thomas Durant, an owner of the Union Pacific, bet Charles Crocker $10,000 that his Central Pacific crew could not lay ten miles of track in one day. Crocker's crew won the bet and Crocker shook the hand of every laborer on the Central Pacific.

When an engineer had to stop unexpectedly, the rear brakeman jumped off the train and ran back for about ½ mile along the track. There he would strap a small torpedo onto the rail. When an oncoming train ran over it, the explosion would warn the engineer to stop immediately.

Wealthy people rode on the plush, comfortable Pullman cars while not-so-well-to-do immigrants rode in "Zulu" cars. They were springless, leaky, crowded cars divided into three groupings: single men in one car; families and single women in another car; Chinese workers traveling to work on the railroad on a third car.

Early train cars had wood-burning stoves at one end to help keep passengers warm. There was also a water tank on each car. Passenger helped themselves to the water and used a cup attached to the cooler by a chain.

The Underground Railroad

Learn about the Underground Railroad by reading the paragraphs below. Complete the activities that follow. For more information about the Underground Railroad you may want to read these books: *The Story of the Underground Railroad* by R. Conrad Stein (Children's Press, 1981) or ... *If you Traveled on the Underground Railroad* by Ellen Levine (Scholastic Inc., 1988).

As early as the 1600's Africans were captured and brought to live as slaves in North America. A few attempted escape from captivity and lived in small colonies in the swamps or forests. Some were accepted by and lived with Native American tribes.

However, not until the time of the Civil War was organized action taken to free the slaves. Some people determined that the best way to abolish slavery was to help the slaves escape to freedom. The Underground Railroad was created. "Conductors" served as guides to lead slaves to shelter at houses called "stations." The owner of the house was the "station master" while the escaping slaves were called "passengers." One of the most famous "conductors" was a Black American—Harriet Tubman. She took more than 300 passengers on rides through the Underground Railroad. Harriet was a clever conductor who employed various tricks and disguises. Often she would dress men in women's clothing and women in men's clothing. Once she hid a group of slaves under a pile of manure and supplied them with straws to breathe through. Slave owners were angry with her and offered total rewards of $40,000 for her capture.

When the Civil War ended, so did the Underground Railroad. On December 6, 1865 the thirteenth amendment to the Constitution was ratified. In one sentence, slavery in the United States of America was abolished.

Activities

- Construct a chart to show the similarities between the Underground Railroad and the regular railroad.

- Write about some other methods conductors used to confuse and trick the slave hunters from tracking and finding fugitives.

- Draw a Wanted poster for Harriet Tubman. Include a sketch, physical descriptions, and the reward.

- Read the thirteenth amendment to the Constitution. Copy it on a clean sheet of paper in your best handwriting.

Important Railroad People

Each of the people listed in the box below has made an important contribution to the railroad industry. Read the descriptions and write the name of the correct person on the lines provided.

Isaac Dripps	Casey Jones	George Westinghouse
Isaac Newton	Eli Janney	George Pullman
John Stevens	Richard Trevithick	Sarah J. Hale
Theodore Judah	Abraham Lincoln	Kate Shelley

1. _____ invented brakes for trains.

2. _____ designed sleeping and private cars.

3. _____ warned an oncoming train of danger ahead.

4. _____ suggested steam-powered vehicles in 1680.

5. _____ greatly promoted a transcontinental railroad.

6. _____ built the first American steam engine.

7. _____ was a legendary, brave engineer.

8. _____ signed a bill to begin building a transcontinental railroad.

9. _____ wrote about poor traveling conditions on trains.

10. _____ developed the cowcatcher for trains.

11. _____ built the first workable self-propelled locomotive.

12. _____ designed automatic couplers for trains cars.

On Your Own: Find out the names of other people who helped build and improve the railroads. Write about their contributions.

Research This

Make a copy of this page and cut apart the research topics on the heavy lines. Place the rectangular pieces into an empty shoe box or lunch bag. Group the students and allow one person from each group to draw one slip of paper. Direct them to research the question and write a two or three paragraph answer and explanation. When all groups have completed their research, share the questions and answers in a whole group setting.

1. Who was Nellie Bly? What book influenced her accomplishment? For whom did she work? How long was her adventure?

2. Casey Jones was a popular engineer on the Illinois Central Railroad. Where was he headed the night of April 29, 1900? Why was he late? Who was Sim Webb?

3. How did Kate Shelly save 200 people? Where did the actual story take place? How old was she?

4. There were no dining cars on early transcontinental trains. Fred Harvey changed all that with his Harvey Girls. Who were they? What did they do?

5. Who was "Crazy Judah"? What was his contribution to the transcontinental railroad? Did he ever see his dream fulfilled?

6. What influence did the ancient Greeks have on modern railroads? What was the ancient Egyptians' contribution to early railroads?

7. How were the railroads used during the Civil War? Why were railroads prime targets by both sides?

8. Who were Frank and Jesse James? What did they have to do with the railroad?

9. John Henry was a black steel driller. What is the legend surrounding his life?

10. Who was Buffalo Bill? What did he have to do with the railroad workers? What "fad" did he start?

Answers for Research This

Listed below are brief answers to the questions on the previous page (Research This, page 67). These are mainly for your reference. Student responses may contain more information than is provided here.

1. Nellie Bly was a reporter for the New York World. She and her editor had been reading Jules Verne's *Around the World in Eighty Days*. She told the editor she could make the journey in 75 days. A train helped her make the journey in only 72 days.

2. John Luther Jones was filling in for an ailing engineer. He left the station 92 minutes late so he and his fireman, Sim Webb, decided to make up for lost time. Almost to their destination, they crashed into a stalled train. Casey died, but Sim managed to jump before the crash.

3. On July 6, 1881 15-year old Kate Shelly heard a crash. She checked it out and in the dark stormy night, crawled to the Moingona, Iowa station. Kate reported the train crash and warned them to stop the oncoming scheduled passenger train.

4. Harvey Girls were 18-30 year-old uniformed waitresses who worked in restaurants established by Fred Harvey along the train routes. They earned $17.50 per month plus tips, room, and board in dormitories. Their curfew was 10 p.m.

5. Theodore Dehone Judah was a civil engineer. He suggested and pushed for a transcontinental railroad. Stagecoach owners hated the idea; it could put them out of business. They called him "Crazy Judah." He died of yellow fever before the transcontinental line was built.

6. Over 2,000 years ago the ancient Greeks built wooden rails on crude roads. The ancient Egyptians invented a crude steam engine 2,100 years ago; no one knew what to do with it. Not until 1698 did Thomas Savery build a workable steam engine.

7. Flatcars hauled heavy mortars and observation balloons. Trains transported troops, arms, and provisions for battle. Both sides were trying to destroy the other's ability to move men and equipment so they were constantly destroying one another's railroad tracks.

8. Frank and Jesse were brothers who had fought as guerrillas for the Confederacy. After the Civil War ended, they formed a gang that robbed banks. In 1873 they began to hold up trains where they took cash and jewelry from passengers.

9. Henry worked for the Chesapeake and Ohio Railroad. Someone bet that John could pound holes in rock deeper and faster than the new steam drills. Using a 30-pound hammer, John succeeded but died as a result.

10. William F. Cody was an ex-Pony Express rider and a hunter hired to shoot buffalo for meat for the railroad workers. He was an excellent shot and earned the nickname Buffalo Bill. It became fashionable to hunt buffalo even from moving trains.

Shape Locomotive

Challenge your students to make a locomotive using only rectangles, triangles, and circles. Give each student (or group of students) a copy of this page. Tell them to cut out the shapes and arrange them on a sheet of black construction paper; glue the pieces to the background. Add details (tracks, smokes, etc.) using white chalk.

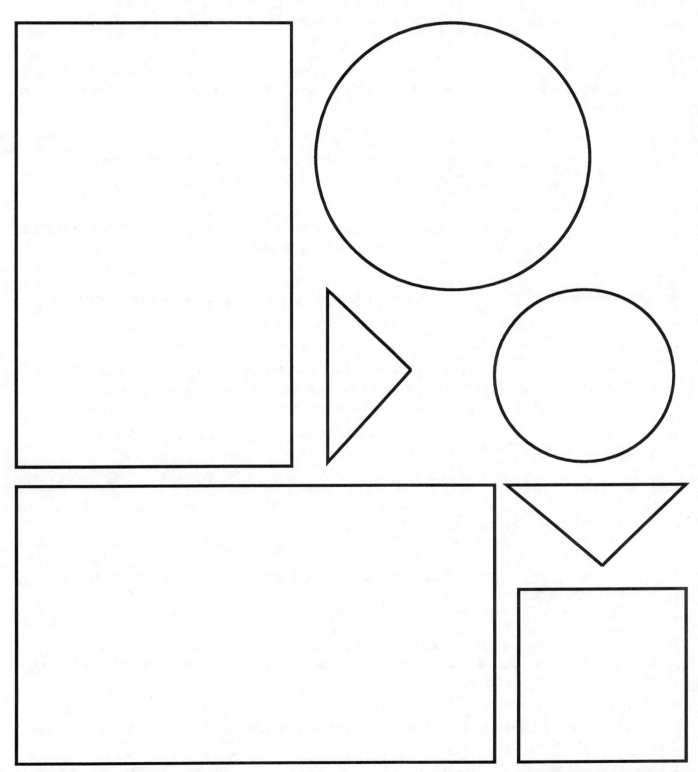

Working on the Railroad

Railroad travel has changed dramatically since the first passenger line opened in the 1830's. Riding has become faster and far more comfortable than in the early days when cars were open and safety features were nonexistent. Dining cars, Pullman cars, and railroad stations added to the ease of riding by rail. Throughout the many changes railroads have undergone in the last century, one thing has remained the same. Smooth train rides require the team work of a variety of jobs. Read about some of these occupations below. Unscramble the name of each worker on the lines provided.

1. The (oducnrotc) _ _ _ _ _ _ _ _ _ supervises the train's operations. From his desk in the caboose he maintains records of all shipments. It is also his responsibility to see that all crew members do their work properly.

2. An (ingerene) _ _ _ _ _ _ _ _ operates the locomotive. From his right hand seat in the engine's cab he watches signals along the track and the gauges inside the compartment.

3. A (merfain) _ _ _ _ _ _ _ is also part of the engine crew. He sits on the left side of the cab and acts as co-pilot as he, too, watches the track signals and engine gauges.

4. The (meknareb) _ _ _ _ _ _ _ _ assist the conductor. Their duties include uncoupling cars and helping with the signals.

5. A (certsdiaph) _ _ _ _ _ _ _ _ _ _ is in charge of all train movements in his territory. He uses an electronic control board to show him a train's position and to dispatch signals to trains.

6. (crtka ngags) _ _ _ _ _   _ _ _ _ _ are responsible for inspecting and keeping the track in good repair.

7. A (admsreyatr) _ _ _ _ _ _ _ _ _ _ is in charge of a railroad "yard" where cars are switched around to make up trains that are going in the same direction.

8. (nmesthciw) _ _ _ _ _ _ _ _ _ work in railroad yards using lists made by the yardmaster to get railroad cards organized into trains.

In addition to these jobs the railroad employs telegraphers, boiler makers, carpenters, electricians. architects, chemists, and even doctors and lawyers. Passenger trains employ baggage handlers, cooks, porters, food servers, and messengers.

There are many more careers that the railroad has to offer. Ask your librarian to help you find out more information about these jobs.

Railroad Songs

The railroad left its mark on American music. Its influence is evident in the words of the songs below. Accompanying music can be found in *Wee Sing America. Songs of Patriots and Pioneers* by Pamela Conn Beall and Susan Hagen Nipp (Price Stern Sloan, Inc., 1987). A cassette tape recording of these songs are also available from the same company. Other sources include: *Tom Glazer's Treasury of Songs for Children* compiled by Tom Glazer (Doubleday, 1969). It is arranged for piano with guitar chords. Also see *Gonna Sing My Head Off! American Folk Songs for Children* collected and arranged by Kathleen Krull (Alfred A. Knopf, 1992). Included are "The Erie Canal," "Casey Jones," and "John Henry."

I've Been Working on the Railroad

I've been working on the railroad, all the live long day.
I've been working on the railroad, just to pass the time away.
Don't you hear the whistle blowin', rise up so early in the morn;
Don't you hear the captain shouting, "Dinah, blow your horn!"
Dinah, won't you blow, Dinah won't you blow, Dinah, won't you blow your horn.
Dinah, won't you blow, Dinah won't you blow, Dinah, won't you blow your horn!
Someone's in the kitchen with Dinah, someone's in the kitchen, I know
Someone's in the kitchen with Dinah, strummin' on the old banjo
And singin' fee fi fiddlee-i-o, fee fi fiddlee-i-o
Fee, fi, fiddlee-i-o, strummin' on the old banjo.

Drill, Ye Tarriers

Ev'ry morning at seven o'clock,
There's twenty tarriers a workin' on the rock,
And the boss comes along and he says, "Keep still,
And come down heavy on the cast iron drill."
Chorus:
And drill ye tarriers, drill. Drill ye tarriers, drill.
For it's work all day for sugar in your tay.
Down beyond the railway
And drill ye tarriers, drill! And blast! And fire!

John Henry

When John Henry was a little baby
Sittin' on his daddy's knee.
He picked up a hammer and a little piece of steel
Said, "This hammer's gonna be the death of me, Lawd, Lawd.
This hammer's gonna be the death of me."

Bulletin Board Ideas

One way to motivate students is through the use of bulletin boards. This page shows you how to get the most from a bulletin board by making it an interactive teaching tool. Patterns for the continental U.S. outline map can be found on pages 73 to 76.

1. Prepare the bulletin board background with colored butcher paper. Make copies of the U.S. outline on pages 73 to 76. Cut around the outline and staple the pieces together onto the background. Use pushpins to highlight the three designated cities. Suggested uses: have students label some important cities along the route; assign a small group to draw and label the states between Omaha and Nebraska; write facts on sticky note, (for example, Chinese laborers made up the bulk of its crew.); direct the students to place the notes under the proper line—Central Pacific or Union Pacific.

2. Assemble the bulletin board pieces on a large sheet of poster board and laminate. Write on the laminated surface with water-based wipe-off pens. Employ any of the suggested uses in #1 above.

3. Trace the outline of the steam engine on page 27. Cut out and place one on each side of the bulletin board. Label one engine Central Pacific and the other engine Union Pacific. Cut strips of black construction paper 1" (2.5 cm) wide; join together to create dividers (see diagram at left). On 3"x5" (7.5 cm x 12.5 cm) index cards write facts about each railroad. Add to it throughout the unit. Use the cards for reviewing information or as flash cards.

4. Enlarge the engine pattern from page 27. (Use an overhead projector or have it done at a copy shop.) Color, if desired, cut out and attach to a bulletin board background. Make a label for each train part—using index cards or cut rectangular pieces of construction paper. Staple a length of yarn next to each part to be identified. Students can work in pairs to paper clip the labels to the correct parts.

5. A ready-made locomotive pattern can be found in Teacher Created Material's #063 *Think and Do Bulletin Boards*.

Continental United States

See directions on page 72. Put map together before gluing to prevent the wrong tabs from being glued.

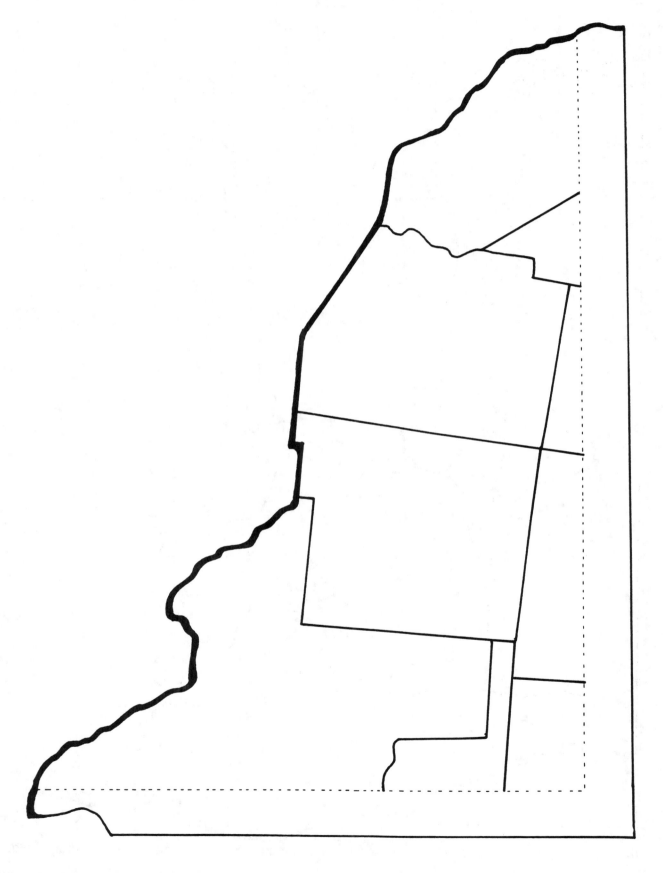

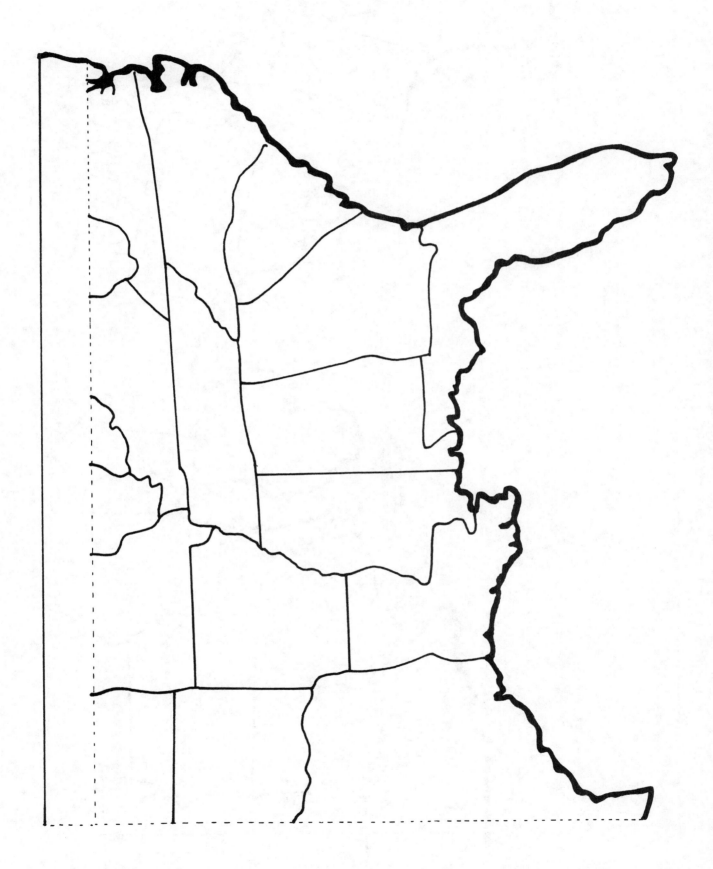

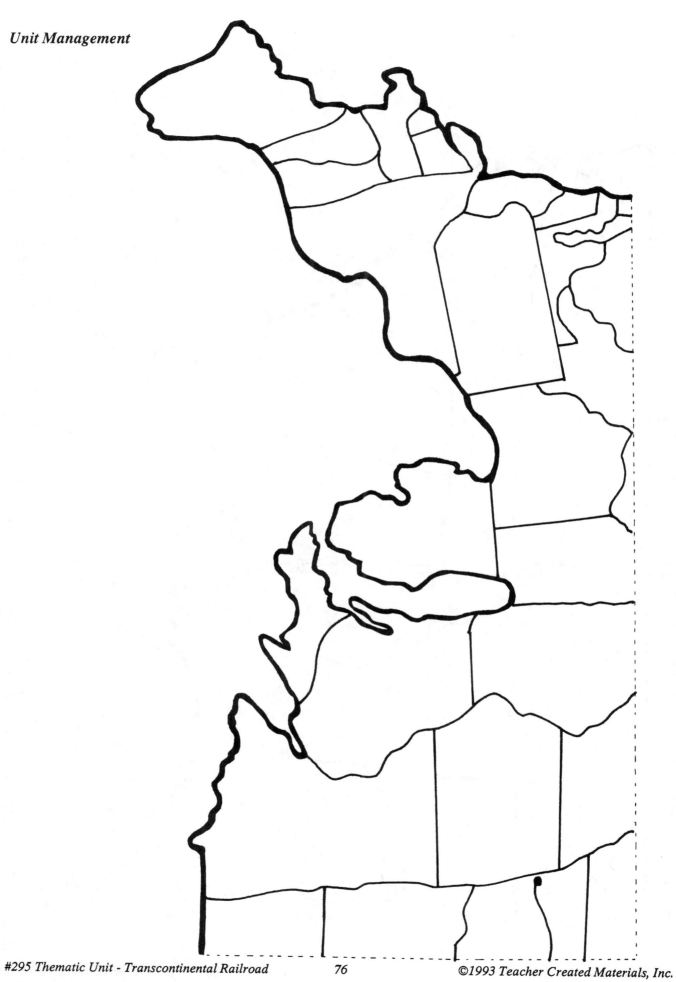

Awards

Use these awards as rewards for turning in homework assignments, winning a class competition, or for reporting achievements. Both patterns below can easily be converted to letters to send home or creative writing shapes. Simply cover the inside of the shape with paper cut to fit. Make a copy on the copier. Leave the inside blank or write a message of your own on the inside before making a copy for each student.

Date

has the right train of thought!

Student's Name

Congratulations on _____

Sincerely,

_____

Teacher's Signature

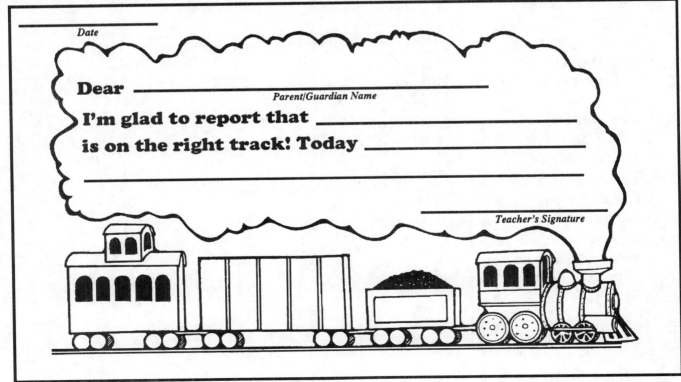

Date

Dear _____

Parent/Guardian Name

I'm glad to report that _____

is on the right track! Today _____

_____

Teacher's Signature

         #295 Thematic Unit - Transcontinental Railroad

Answer Key

page 12

Engines: steam; diesel; electric; jet

Safety Devices: air brakes; cowcatcher; steam whistle; couplers

Crew Members: engineer; flagman; fireman; brakeman

Railroad Lines: Southern Pacific; Erie; Santa Fe; Baltimore & Ohio

page 13

Answers may vary. Check for appropriateness.

page 19

1. They wanted the land for themselves. They attacked and burned tipi villages.

2. They had great fun tying cloth to ponies' tails, stepping on the cloth to try to jerk the riders out of their saddles.

3. They took coins for the women and gathered precious things to bring back to the tribe.

4. They described it as breathing out smoke, having the voice of thunder.

5. Only three men manned the train and no military escort accompanied it.

6. They shot arrows at it and tried to rope it despite their terrified horses.

7. Another train was seen in the distance.

8. They were armed only with bows and arrows, knives, and tomahawks.

page 20

Possible Answers:

2. Sol: People fought back bravely to protect themselves.

   Re: They lived in fear of more attacks.

3. Sol: They must cut them apart to set her free.

   Re: They chopped ties in the middle and hacked out spikes.

4. Sol: They knocked off the lock.

   Re: They kept the coins and threw away the paper money.

5. Sol: They set the boxcars on fire.

   Re: They thought their people would no longer fear the Iron Horse.

page 23

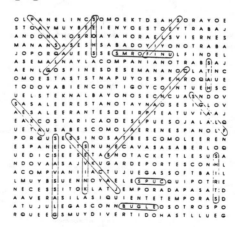

page 24

3 - 11 - 6 - 14 - 1 - 18 - 5 - 13
8 - 17 - 2 - 16 - 9 - 4 - 12 -
10 - 7 - 15

page 27

page 28

1. First, coal is placed...
2. Above the firebox...
3. Heat turns the...
4. The resulting steam...
5. From the steam dome...
6. Once inside the...
7. The drive rod...
8. Movement of the...

page 40

1. canal
2. cowcatcher
3. famine
4. emigrated
5. gauge
6. certificates
7. facilitated
8. impede
9. allies
10. modest
11. optimistic
12. charter

page 41

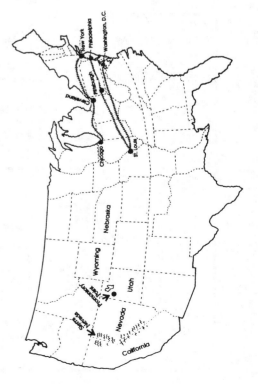

Answer Key *(cont.)*

page 43
1. 6 years
2. $6/$ .43 per hour
3. 27,182 miles
4. 1,300 miles
5. 83 each day
6. $68,000
7. 20,833 shares
8. 10,000 more
9. 200,000 pounds
10. $20,000
11. 12,999,517
12. 1,500,000

page 44
1. $720.00
2. 6 pounds
3. $6.85
4. 6 cents
5. 16
6. $11.25
7. 20 cents
8. $370.00
9. $53.20
10. $89.00
11. $1,067.55
12. 200 pound rice

page 45
Chinese: 1,2,8,10,13
Both: 3,6,9,14
Irish: 4,5,7,11,12

page 46
1. C   6. U   11. C
2. C   7. C   12. U
3. U   8. C   13. C
4. C   9. U   14. C
5. U   10. U   15. C

page 47
1. few people rode...
2. numerous accidents...
3. the value of its...
4. future profits...
5. Peter Dey...
6. rates were kept...
7. railroads became...
8. the careers...
9. it couldn't be...
10. public sympathized...

page 52
Crossword Puzzle

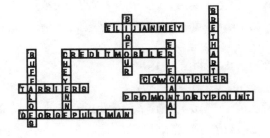

page 55
1. 4-8-4 Northern
2. 2-6-0 Mogul
3. 2-10-0 Decapod
4. 2-10-2 Santa Fe
5. 4-6-4 Hudson
6. 2-8-2 Mikado

page 56
1. 112,500,000
2. 6 ½ hours
3. 2,150
4. 22,280
5. 7
6. 30 hours

page 57
1. <   6. >
2. <   7. <
3. >   8. <
4. <   9. <
5. >   10. >

page 58
1. Stourbridge Lion
2. Rocket
3. New Tokaido
4. Mallard
5. APT
6. Turbotrain
7. Hovertrain
8. Linear Motor Car
2. 290 miles per hour
3. 208.75 miles per hour
4. 220 miles per hour
5. 79 miles per hour

page 59
Time Zones
1. Answers will vary 2. 10 a.m.
3. 11 p.m. 4. 3 a.m. 5. 7 p.m.

page 62
Freight Cars

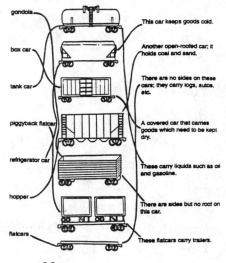

page 66
1. George Westinghouse
2. George Pullman
3. Kate Shelley
4. Isaac Newton
5. Theodore Judah
6. John Stevens
7. Casey Jones
8. Abraham Lincoln
9. Sarah J. Hale
10. Isaac Dripps
11. Richard Trevithick
12. Eli Janney

page 69

page 70
1. conductor   4. brakemen
2. engineer   5. dispatcher
3. fireman   6. track gangs
7. yardmaster   8. switchmen

Bibliography

Historical Fiction

Botkins, B.A. and Alvin F. Harlow, editors. *A Treasury of Railroad Folklore*. Bonanza Books, 1953.

Fraser, Mary Ann. *Ten Mile Day and the Building of the Transcontinental Railroad*. Henry Holt, 1993.

Goble, Paul. *Death of the Iron Horse*. Bradbury, 1987.

Keats, Ezra Jack. *John Henry*. Dragonfly Books, 1965.

Quackenbush, Robert. *She'll Be Comin' Round the Mountain*. Harper Collins, 1988.

Wetterer, Margaret K. *Kate Shelly and the Midnight Express*. Carolrhoda Books, 1990.

Nonfiction

Brown, Dee. *Hear That Lonesome Whistle Blow: Railroads in the West*. Holt, 1977.

Elting, Mary. *All Aboard! The Railroad Trains That Built America*. Four Winds Press, 1951.

Fisher, Leonard Everett. *Tracks Across America*. Holiday House, 1992.

Harvey T. *Railroads*. Lerner Publications Company, 1980.

Hilton, Suzanne. *Faster Than a Horse: Moving West With Engine Power*. Westminster, 1983.

Latham, Frank B. *The Transcontinental Railroad*. Franklin Watts, 1973.

Levine, Ellen. *If You Traveled on the Underground Railroad*. Scholastic, 1988.

McCague, James. *When the Rails Ran West*. Garrard Publishing Company, 1967.

Miller, Marilyn. *The Transcontinental Railroad*. Silver Burdett, 1986.

Nathan, Adele. *The Building of the First Transcontinental Railroad*. Franklin Watts, 1973.

Retan, Walter. *The Big Book of Real Trains*. Grosset & Dunlap, 1987.

Rutland, Jonathan. *The Young Engineer Book of Supertrains*. Usborne Publishing, 1978.

Scarry, Huck. *Aboard a Steam Locomotive*. Prentice-Hall, 1987.

Stein R. Conrad. *The Story of the Golden Spike*. Children's Press, 1978.

The Story of the Underground Railroad. Children's Press, 1981.

Wood, Sydney. *Trains and Railroads*. Dorling Kindersley, 1992.

Yepsin, Roger. *Train Talk,* Pantheon Books, 1983.

Poetry

Bennett, Jill, collected by. *Noisy Poems*. Oxford University Press, 1987.

Hopkins, Lee Bennett, selected by. **Click, Rumble, Roar**. Thomas Y. Crowell, 1983.

Teacher Created Materials

#063 *Think and Do Bulletin Boards*

#133 *Making Big and Little Books*

#282 *Westward Ho* (Thematic Unit)

#285 *Native Americans* Intermediate (Thematic Unit)

#804 *United States* (Jumbo Note Pad)